This book is dedicated to Laura Rojo and her daughters,
Laura, Nellie, and Nancy.

Contents

Why This Book

"When you pass strangers on the street, the unfamiliar faces blur. When you let your lives touch and make the effort of asking questions and listening to the stories they tell, you discover the intricate patterns of their differences, and at the same time, the underlying themes that all members of our species have in common."

—*Mary Catherine Bateson*

When I look into the faces of my students, faces that come from all over the globe, I realize that the most important task at hand as a teacher is to understand each student's reality. In other words, I need to know who the student is and what knowledge of American English culture is present. Then, how does this new knowledge interact with that of the home culture? What attitudes do the students have that might affect the acquisition of a second language? What social and familial influences are there?

All of these questions can be answered if I know the student's story, the cultural and individual journey that has been undertaken so far. In order to better understand their journey, on the first day of class, I encourage students to write their own stories. Sometimes I ask them to interview each other and write each other's stories. Often it isn't easy, but gradually their stories unfold. The stories are fascinating to read and hear, and I always learn something I didn't know. Knowing their stories, as I begin to understand their identities, I begin to connect with the students and teach them English as a second language in a meaningful way. I am teaching a real human being, not a stereotype or abstraction, and suddenly all sorts of possibilities exist for the students' achievements in a second language.

There are many books written describing the odyssey into the foreign land and the experience of learning a second language. One author, Eva Hoffman, who emigrated from Poland as an adolescent, wrote in her memoir, *Lost in Translation* (Penguin Books, 1989):

> *Everyday I learn new words, new expressions, I pick them up from school exercises, from conversations, from the books I take out of Vancouver's well-lit, cheerful public library. There are some turns of phrase to which I develop strange allergies. "You're welcome," for example, strikes me as a gaucherie, and I can hardly bring myself to say it—I suppose because it implies that there's something to be thanked for, which in Polish would be impolite. The very places where language is at its most conventional, where it should be most taken for granted, are the places where I feel the prick of artifice.*
>
> *Then there are the words to which I take an equally irrational liking, for their sound, or just because I'm pleased to have deduced their meaning. Mainly they're words I learn from books, like "enigmatic" or "insolent"— words that have only a literary value, that exist only as signs on the page.*
>
> *But, mostly, the problem is that the signifier has become severed from the signified. The words I learn now don't stand for things in the same unquestioned way they did in my native tongue. "River" in Polish was a vital sound, energized with the essence of riverhood, of my rivers, of my being immersed in rivers. "River" in English is cold—a word without an aura. It has no accumulated associations for me, and it does not give off the radiating haze of connotation. It does not evoke. (p. 106)*

In this excerpt, much is conveyed about teaching English as a second language, about the importance of having students write personal narratives in order to be able to learn to use words in a familiar context. In other words, I would let the young Eva as a student of English write about the rivers in Poland, a landscape that is meaningful to her, before I ask her to write about rivers in a more abstract sense. I would also help her put words in context from her "literary" assignments. I might teach her word-building skills to help her become better grounded in vocabulary. All of this would happen because I connected with her story and, in particular, about the acquisition of language and culture.

I have discovered that narratives can suggest powerful ways of learning about effective teaching because they focus on the student's perspective. I have discussed how important identity is in my earlier book, *Lives in Two Languages* (University of Michigan Press, 2001). *Understanding Cultural Narratives* continues the discussion of identity but focuses on narrative as a means of revealing it.

Furthermore, when I teach ESL bilingual teacher-training courses, I have rarely found a topic as compelling as that of the cross-cultural story. The narrative as a tool for learning is part of an important paradigm in the sociocultural theory. My graduate students will learn about narrative and its history in the social sciences as an introduction to studying cross-cultural stories. But it is when the graduate students in my classes read an actual account about a border-crossing, in which the individual's narrative documents the shift in perspective and the identity revision that accompanies it, that they finally understand the issues, problems, and enrichment that confront the bilingual individual as he or she changes gradually over a period of time. Furthermore, I have found that when we read texts from stories and poems that illustrate this journey, students respond with stories of identity of their own. Suddenly, an "aha" moment exists. The teacher trainees see a connection between their stories and the stories of people from other cultures. Where there previously was stereotyping, there is now an understanding of the immigrant as a person. An important feature of narratives is the recognition of the similarity that human beings have in the effort to gain agency or control over their lives. And yet, at the same time, this ability to cope, to be successful, exists in a cultural context that may not always be obvious to the observer.

If you have never moved from the very place you were born or never had to make sense out of an alien word, it is difficult to understand what the fuss is about. If someone has even moved from one part of the same country, state, or city to another part either near or far, there had to be an accompanying shift in perspective. Identities change in any new context, even going away to college, even when there is no language barrier. Therefore, for people who cross boundaries into countries, the adjustment is more intense, with learning a new language part of that experience. Language is learned in context and reflects the experience of the learner. In fact, Chapters 2–4 explore literature and poetry as a means of uncovering stories about identity.

One effective tool for exploration of this area of inquiry is the ethnographic interview, a carefully controlled and documented question-and-answer process that has been an integral part of the qualitative research paradigm of the social sciences. It is essential that teacher trainees understand their own identities so that they can understand identity issues of others. Yet, many English-dominant people are not firmly grounded on their own cultural trappings, even if they are vestigial and handed down from many generations. Even I, whose ancestors first set foot in North America 400 years ago, have become gradually more aware of language, both words and pronunciation, and traditions that go back to the area around Lancaster, England, through teaching and learning about ethnography and the ethnographic interview. Cultural anthropologists tell us that much of cultural tradition and behavior is unconscious (Geertz, 2000). It is through the understanding of these cultural behaviors that we begin to perceive our own authentic identities.

In my graduate class, when we study the transcripts of ethnographic interviews, we become aware of the power of narrative and the power that comes with learning to discover each person's unique story. We soon see that we are all a part of the same human community on this fragile planet. In sharing a student's narrative, the teacher-trainers learn about each other, the similarities and differences. Self-discovery helps students gain the ability to be self-determining in a new milieu. When they understand who they are, they gain the same or greater control over their lives as when they were on familiar ground. This kind of knowledge has tremendous positive consequences for an individual; it brings empowerment. When students articulate answers in an interview, feelings of loss and vulnerability seem less threatening. For us as teachers, greater understanding of bilingual or multicultural individuals results from an emphasis on the narratives of real-life stories that chronicle the adjustments and choices made in a new milieu. It is important to remember this fact: *No matter how wonderful the pedagogical plan is, without connecting with the student through understanding his or her narrative, the lesson will not be as effective, and even might be totally misdirected. Through connection, meaning is made. Nothing is truly learned without a meaningful context.*

Besides the obvious benefits for their students, another important benefit that resulted from this approach to teacher training has been the opportunity for writing that the ethnographic interview, by its very nature, requires from teacher trainees. Many graduate students come to their classes lacking recent practice in writing the sort of lengthy research projects that are required in most graduate programs. Using this reading-writing approach with ethnographic interview has helped students to gain control over their writing processes once again. In fact, interviews have led to embracing other methods of the ethnographic method of research, and even doctoral dissertations. The stories that were unearthed were so compelling that students found themselves carried along effortlessly in a tide of narrative. Most important, they were excited about learning in ways that helped them discover their identities as writers, educators, and researchers. The ethnographic interview and summaries are explored in Chapters 6 and 7.

My hope is that, as a result of using this text to understand narration as a mode of inquiry and through reading poetry, literature, and ethnography that evokes exploration of the self and identity, students will become transformed into effective teachers who are able to connect more deeply with the students they teach.

CHAPTER 1

Sociocultural Theory and Narrative

This book examines second language acquisition (SLA) and culture acquisition, but not in the usual sense where the lexical, grammatical, and semantic systems are learned or acquired. Rather, it is about the attempt to adapt the self into a new context and a new world. It is about the struggle for participation in a new social environment. Participation has emerged in the SLA literature as a metaphor for learning a new language. The background for this model stems from sociohistorical and social constructionist theories; participation in society as described by the individual's narrative can be interpreted as a metaphor for acquiring a new identity (Sfard, 1998; Pavlenko and Lantolf, 2000).

SLA and acculturation can be accurately described as participation and reconstruction of the self. It is more than the individual becoming a repository of new knowledge. Participation is more effective as a way to think about language socialization because it connotes interactive communication between the learner and the new community, the way it occurs in the real world. As a complement to the older acquisition metaphor, participation as expressed in the form of the narrative is particularly appropriate. The roots of this theory can be found in the writings of Vygotsky (1978) in his theory of language learning as social interaction, as inner speech converted into outer. Interaction comes to play in Bakhtin's (1981) focus on identity in his discussion of the dialogic, the idea that a person can have different languages depending on the context, and that language, culture, and identity are fluid, dynamic processes.

Traditional scientific understanding has been based on the establishment of laws or patterns that exist across contexts, as a deductive system of reasoning that is rule-based and thus independent of the forces of the environment in which the phenomenon exists. While this is a valid paradigm of research, it is best complemented by narrative-based research, which like its linearly logical, mathematical counterpart, also addresses issues of validity and reliability. Furthermore, narrative-based research is more appropriate in studying human behaviors and activities because of the nature of the subject. To study human beings is in many ways more complex than studying phenomena in the physical world because a human being is more complicated than a rock or a kind of gas (Polkinghorne, 1998, p. 10).

At the heart of narrative research or anthropological inquiry rest the intention and the integrity of the researcher. This kind of investigation is not for everyone. Those who are uncomfortable with loose ends, with participation and interview as a kind of "deep hanging out" (Geertz, 2000), and the "holistic" view of things will not find themselves comfortable with narrative research. Those who need structure to be comfortable with research will find themselves better off using a more empirical or statistical method that has its roots in the traditional scientific method. Furthermore, it has long been a controversial fact for professionals in the scientific community that a form of research exists that relies on the personal factor in which the main form of research is socializing and the main instrument is the researcher. And yet in many ways, this form of research presents a "real picture of reality, of life as it exists in time and space" (Neisser, 1976, p. 2). And a careful researcher structures and triangulates the data so that this method has its own kind of rigor.

For research into acculturation and identity, the narrative form of research is an appropriate tool. To better understand this form of research, we shall first explore the writings of two researchers previously mentioned whose work has been essential in moving the importance of *context* to the center of concerns in acculturation research and second language acquisition: Lev Vygotsky and Mikhail Bakhtin. In addition, the ideas of Jerome Bruner, who questioned empiricism as the only method of viewing phenomena, are all examined.

Lev Vygotsky (1978), influenced by Marxist theory, claimed that higher mental functioning stemmed from the individual's participation in society. He believed that in order to understand the individual, one must study the social context. Higher mental functions are social and reflect on the individual's social interaction. Even internal mental functions are the result on some level of social interaction. The clearest manifestation of this idea can be seen in the idea of the "zone of proximal development"; that is, in education, we should teach to the student's potential, not just the actual level in which the individual is functioning. This theory speaks to identity and interaction and moves language learning out of the abstract, isolated internal mental functioning into the real world of human communication (Wertsch, 1991, p. 28).

Mikhail Bakhtin (1981) gave new meaning to the act of communication by focusing on the dialogic aspect—that is, in any given text there is more than one voice. This makes a text not a passive receptacle, but a generator of meaning. Each text is subject to a continual stream of meanings, depending on who is creating it and who the reader or audience is. Any single text is subject to interpretation of the speaker and listener or reader and writer. An example of this theory can be seen in the responses to interviews in Carol Gilligan's book, *In a Different Voice* (1993), where the interviewer's questions are at times misinterpreted by the women interviewed. Gilligan claimed that women can see meaning in interview questions that men cannot. In this way, the dialogic aspect of text makes it open to more than one meaning or interpretation, all of which are culturally and socially influenced. Another example of finding different results due to differing interpretations can be seen in Margaret Donaldson's study (1978) of children's performances in Piagetian tasks in which children performed a task (let's allow the task be the text since these children do not read yet) successfully at an earlier stage than Piaget had found in the original study. She argued that in Piaget's study the children didn't really understand the task because when given a similar task in a more familiar context, they performed correctly. Similarly, children across cultures can interpret any given task differently. A good way to understand Bakhtin's point of view is to raise the question "Who is doing the talking?" and expect more than one answer to the question (Wertsch, 1991, p. 53).

Jerome Bruner (1991) felt that the perceptions people hold and the way they make sense of their worlds could not be a testable proposition, like that found in the empirical sciences. He was instrumental in introducing narrative-based research into psychology. He posited that there was more than one way to order experience and construct reality. He was following the line of reasoning of George Mead (1977), who felt that people themselves played an active role in constructing their own lives and that their interpretations could be organized into a methodology. However, none of these pioneering thinkers were advocating one research method as better than another. As Polkinghorne, a professor of counseling and psychology, said:

> *I do not believe that the solutions to human problems will come from developing even more sophisticated creative applications of the natural science model, but by developing additional, complementary approaches that are especially sensitive to the unique characteristics of human existence (1988, p. x).*

To summarize then, narrative, especially first-person singular narrative, has been very much marginalized by the social sciences until recently because the social scientists have used the empirical scientific paradigm as a model. For many, the only way of knowing and research is extreme objectivity where the focus is on the observed, not the observer. There have been exceptions, such as the introspective case studies in SLA of Schumann and Schumann (1977). For the most part, however, linguistics has modeled itself after the rationalist epistemology and experimental methodology of the hard sciences.

I believe that first-person singular narrative voice provides a rich template through which to observe human interaction and behavior. Retroactive first-person narrative should be moved front and center, along with the empirical research that it complements. Authentic autobiography is a manifestation of this kind of knowledge. However, it is also true that narrative written in third person (or "close third" such as in Jhumpa Lahiri's *The Namesake*), where the reader enters the writer's world, also can give an authentic picture of evolving identity in a multicultural world.

Poetry that gives a multi-faced reality of people who have changed contexts and identities is also included. There is, in fact, a continuum—from the artistic like poetry and fiction, to the more scientific ethnography in which to discover identity and shifting perspectives of the multi-cultural world, and we will explore these in this book.

Questions for Discussion and Writing

1. What exactly is narrative-based research?
2. How does it differ from traditional scientific inquiry?
3. What researchers led the way to this kind of research?
4. Who should do narrative-based research, and who would be better off using the scientific method?
5. Why is narrative-based research particularly important in acculturation, second language, and identity research?
6. Write a brief summary of the preceding point of view.

CHAPTER 2

Literature, Narrative, and Identity

As human beings, we are creating narratives as we live our lives. This may be at the subconscious level, but if the story we are forming is more coherent and whole, as opposed to fragmented and split into parts representing different facets of the identity, the story of the self will show integration and healthy adaptation. As Akthar (1993) pointed out in *Lives in Two Languages* (Watkins-Goffman, 2001), this is the ideal, the goal of an acculturated personality, one that is enriched by two cultures and often, two languages. This can be a resource both for personal development and financial gains. On the other hand, the neurotic, alienated personality can often see the future as hopeless and full of loss as is often the case for individuals who have relocated from one culture or subculture to another. There is no doubt that fate intervenes in every personal story, and yet, if we examine the lives of individuals who have a happy life, they have made choices that lead to wholeness and optimism, whether they have moved from one city to another in the same country or from one country to another. Today there are many autobiographies and memoirs of bicultural writers who, even though they had to go through the losses and crises of having to move, have made positive choices. One excellent example as shown in the Why This Book section, is *Lost in Translation* by Eva Hoffman (1989), which I highly recommend having students read in its entirety. Excerpts from other similar stories will be discussed in this text.

In addition to making choices that affect the future, individuals can revise their own stories retrospectively. As they become conscious of their own stories, they can re-order or selectively choose to forget past experiences. In this sense, memoirs can be seen as part fiction and part fact (Conway, 1999). For example, in the acculturation process, individuals often tend to compensate by romanticizing one culture while giving less status to the other as they adapt to living in a new environment. Researchers point to the fact that, for some people, their constructed narratives end before their actual lives end (Shiebe in Polkinghorne, 1988, p. 106). Perhaps this idea could be extended to identity, in that a person can decide to end one identity while keeping the other thriving. This is often seen in cases of unbalanced bilingualism (Hakuta, 1981, p. 95) in which the first or second language is weaker than the other, which can reflect the speaker's feelings about the identity that language evokes.

How is it, then, that we learn the ability to construct narratives as a way to self-discovery and understanding? The history of the attempt to understand this competence follows the history of the development of language and epistemology. Along with understanding the acquisition of language, questions had to be answered, such as "What is the nature of narrative discourse?" and "What is the process by which children learn narrative competence?" Also, "What is narrative knowing or narration as a way of knowing and thinking?"

Cognitive psychologists like Mead (1977) believe that this innate propensity for language is combined with the development of cognition. Narrative knowing, according to Polkinghorne (1988), is the ability to structure information within the schematic knowledge format. Beginning with Aristotle's time, stories seemed to have ingredients such as plot, setting, narrator, and characters. Stories had to have a beginning, a middle, and an end, and they had to represent a sequential kind of knowledge in which the whole is greater than the individual parts. Stories help human beings organize their world temporally in any given framework of time and give them ways to reorder experience.

Within a time experience, a story that can include multiple narratives can explore causality. In this way, causality is a way of understanding human experience and knowledge. Along with other categories of knowledge, such as categorical, taxonomic, and matrix, narrative offers schematic and sequential knowledge. Together, all categories can give ways of organizing human experience and knowledge (Polkinghorne, p. 183).

Levi-Strauss (1958) developed the idea that narrative structures are universally inherent. Most children, regardless of their culture, will even recognize a story from a setting different from one they know. Following this theory of the innatism of language, Noam Chomsky (1972) believed that children have native language competency hard-wired into their brains, and therefore the competence for forming narratives. Kemper (1984) and Piaget (1952) have analyzed children's stories and found they learn storytelling as one of their first language skills. The stories, most of which are dyadic (consisting of two characters) and contain some violence, gain in complexity as the children grow older, reaching the most complexity by age eleven.

This complexity continues until adulthood. We know that narrative helps us understand our world, and relationships and patterns can be discerned by stories. Sometimes it is the context or culture that gives us archetypal scripts that make their way into our stories (Conway, 1999). For example, gender differences in cultures can help us understand women's stories more accurately since very often women write in a male-dominated culture. In fact, until the twentieth century, women's voices have not been heard as often as men's literature and story-telling, making it difficult to understand women's perspectives. And context does affect the meaning of a narration (Conway, 1999, p. 14–17). Even in tales of exploration, women explorers' narratives were often overlooked. The adventurer Mary Kingsley, while she was a popular lecturer in her time, never enjoyed the fame of a Kipling or even Sir Richard Burton (Conway, 1999, p. 65). In order for there to be meaning, it is important to understand the context in which a narrative is told.

Narrative helps us organize our experience and discern patterns and the actions involved in a story. Temporality, a short amount of time, can be organized into categories that show how action is interpreted. Action can be intrinsically meaningful, socially based, or emotionally expressed. Action is a hermeneutical expression of culture and exists in context. Other cultural expressions can include social customs such as food preparation or family traditions. Our human concept of time can provide a context that can be universal time or the human life span with birth and death as markers.

How does narrative inform the concept of self and identity? The concept of self is complex with many components. As early as the 1600s,

Descartes developed the idea that the self exists beyond the corporeal (Cottingham, 1992). The concept of self is further extended to include the social self, according to Erving Goffman (1978). The social self is determined by the role we play and is governed by our interaction with society. It can be, for example, public or private, depending on whether we are with intimates or strangers. Richard Rodriguez explores this concept in his autobiography *Hunger of Memory*. In his story, the intimate or private self becomes his public self through education and acculturation.

Part of the context is the media. In North American culture, novels, movies, plays, and television influence our story-telling, including our personal life stories that we are living. But though the self is reflected in a story, it is also more than a story; it is influenced by who we think we are, including lies we tell ourselves. Sometimes who we are is revealed not by what is in our stories, but by what is left out of them or what is distorted about our true identities, that which is exaggerated or false. According to psychologist Goleman (1985), we often tell ourselves lies in order to be able to survive. Some acts of great heroism have been the results of self-deception in which an ordinary person can convince oneself that there is no danger despite incredible odds. Sometimes the truth is too self-destructive so that lying becomes a strategy for self protection. He says that even a three-year-old will edit his rejecting mother out of his perception when she is present in the room because to acknowledge her presence is too painful (p. 47).

These stories can be quite elaborate depending on how creative the individual is and whether the individual is healthy or neurotic, such as the mother who invents a story for the teenage daughter about her life as an insurance salesperson when she is really a prostitute in order to preserve her role of respected caregiver (Goleman, 1985, p. 245). Psychological strategies can be used as defense mechanisms to keep us from facing the truth and the accompanying anxiety. Sometimes we create twists in our identity automatically by suppressing information to the subconscious. Goleman (1985, pp. 120–121) discusses how feelings of rage can be suppressed to the subconscious, then reversed by using projection (putting the feelings into someone else), rationalization, inventing convincing excuses, or sublimation (replacing the destructive impulse with the constructive, i.e., someone who would be a thief goes into banking instead). According to Goleman, self-deception, if it is used minimally, may be necessary in the way humans create their self-identity and weave their stories.

The extent to which we can consciously change the story in order to lead peaceful and connected lives is important. When we read such stories in which there is self-direction and self-fulfillment, we are fascinated and instructed. In many cases, the way in which we take action and display agency in our own life stories will be modeled on the choices we see others make that will determine whether there is a positive result or not. In these stories, an identity can be changed or added to with life-enhancing results. In other words, the way we tell our stories tells a lot about who we think we really are.

Literature and the act of reading together can influence the reader's identity. In *Reading Lolita in Tehran,* Nafisi (2004) discusses the significant role that a reading group had on her students and how the literature changed their experience. The students went to her apartment to read Nabokov's *Lolita*—among other Western novels—in Tehran at a time when teachers were not allowed to teach literature from the western classical canon. Through reading, they were able to enter a whole different world, one with which they were not familiar. There the women students took off their robes, both literally and figuratively. They felt free to express themselves within the walls of Professor Nafisi's apartment and try on other identities. For them, reading was a transformative experience.

Sometimes context can play a role in meaning making. Sociologist Mernissi (2001) feels that the West misunderstands the meaning of the legend of Scheherazade, the heroine who in order to save her life told stories to the king who finally abandoned his plans to behead her due to his attraction to her stories. In *Scheherazade Goes West*, Mernissi says that the story is about a woman remaining calm and clearheaded in the face of danger and consequently becoming more powerful than her king. This is different from the more popular interpretation of Scheherazade as victim. Translating from the original Arabic, Mernissi explains how influential the story has become in helping women attain more equal status in many Islamic societies. Each of these examples attests to the transforming power of literature and the significant role a story can play in one's self discovery and development.

In this book we will be examining excerpts from stories that demonstrate how choices can affect one's identity and life story, as exemplified in fiction and ethnography. We will also explore how choices that were made by others or circumstances beyond our control can have great consequences in the life story.

Questions for Discussion and Writing.

1. What is the goal, the ideal, of an acculturated personality and how can this be reached?
2. How can individuals revise their own stories?
3. What is "narrative knowing," according to Polkinghorne (1988)?
4. What do we learn about narratives from children's storytelling?
5. How is context important in making meaning from narratives? Give some examples from the previous chapter.
6. How do people twist and distort the truth in storytelling, according to Goleman?
7. How can we, as educators, use stories and story-telling to help us understand our students' identities?

CHAPTER 3

How We Learn from Stories

Humans beings learn to form their own stories and discover their own identities based on reading and experiencing other people's stories vicariously. In recent years, a number of stories have been written by immigrants and border crossers, writing in their second language and in the first-person singular of their experience going from their place of birth to a new place. What do we learn from these narratives or stories? To begin this text, we will examine some underlying principles that these stories seem to have in common.

First, there is loss: loss of identity, loss of language, loss of self. To understand what this loss means, we need to understand the nature of the *self*. It is a coherent but dynamic system of perceptions that is constantly in production and emerges as the individual practices with society. These perceptions and activities reflect the history of a group or groups of people and are learned unconsciously by children. They can be displaced by time and space, and transmuted. In addition, the sense of agency is effected, the facility with which an individual interacts and gains control of his or her world. This can be displaced when a person moves from one set of practices to another.

Writing can provide a kind of meta-knowledge from which the writer explores the social identity, even to the point of border-crossing in a kind of virtual reality, the world of literature. Reading texts that reflect writers' identities in a context can provide a point of departure for rich discussion that can lead the participants to discover new identities and new worlds. The excerpts from narratives we will examine in this text will demonstrate how the individual is, to a large extent, in charge of her or his own identity. The extent of the acquisition of a new language and culture can be determined by the individual, and loss can be compensated by a richness of perspective and an experience that is more fully lived from a variety of points of view. The narrative enables us to see signposts along the way where the individual made conscious choices that influenced the manner and the speed of the unfolding new identity or identities (Pavlenko and Lantolf, 2000, p. 156). Some bilingual writers have chronicled the sense of loss of one's personal history, the indigenous part of one's identity. In his desire to reconnect with his native Quechua, for example, Roncalla writes after he has studied English in the United States and has gone back to Peru,

> *During the first weeks in the Andes I had to relearn my Quechua because I was in the Acacia area. My Apurimac dialect was different. I also had to prove that I was an Andean because nobody believed such a tall guy could speak Quechua. Apart from the general goal of the research, my own interest was personal: a deep reconnection with my Andean self and with the culture, landscape, people, and music that I had been longing for (in Ogulnick, 2000, p. 64).*

Self-esteem can be lost as a result of classism and racism. In an interview about racism, the poet Louis Reyes Rivera says:

> *And interestingly enough, of all the 'Latino-Americans' living in the United States, Puerto Ricans and Dominicans—second generation— more easily identify with the Afro-United States scene than with the Anglo-United States scene. And that's not only because of the similarity in music but also because of the similarity in spirit and in social conditions. It's not just a cultural thing, it's an ethnic recognition. And it's a social response to similar conditions (Fernandez, p. 129).*

This seemed to explain why so often I have found students use expressions and idioms from African-American communities (some call this "street English"). The language shows the sense of identification that Rivera mentioned. For many, however, border-crossing can mean loss of perception and inner speech. In describing her search for her Yiddish identity, Mimi Bluestone in *Ogulnick* (2000) wrote:

> *There are times when I become discouraged and wonder why I want to learn Yiddish at all when most of its contemporary speakers are extremely Orthodox Jews with whom I have virtually nothing in common. Or why it is that I want to spend so much time rummaging in the remains of what poet Jacob Glatstein called "an abandoned culture" (quoted in Howe, 1976, p. 452). Abandoned, yes and murdered and silenced (Ogulnick, 2000, p. 78).*

Yiddish was this writer's inner speech, her way of identifying herself with her community. Yet many who speak it have a culture apart from their own even though they have common origins.

Julia Alvarez says about her inner self as expressed in her writing:

> *No, I am not a Dominican writer or really a Dominican in the traditional sense. I don't live on the Island, breathing its daily smells, enduring its particular burdens, speaking its special dominicano. In fact, I would tell a different story and write poems with a different rhythm if I lived and worked there, ate there, made love there, voted there, dried my tears there, laughed my laughter there. Fundamentally what I heard was Ay instead of Oh, if instead of that limited palette of colors in Vermont, gray softening into green, what I saw were colors so bright I'd have to look twice at things to believe that they were real.*

> *But you're right, I'm also not una norteamericana. I am not a mainstream American writer with my roots in a small town in Illinois or Kentucky or even Nuevo Mexico. I don't hear the same rhythms in English as a native speaker of English. Sometimes I hear Spanish in English (and of course, vice versa). That's not just a term. I'm mapping a country that's not on the map, and that's why I'm trying to put it down on paper (Alvarez, 1998, p. 172–173).*

Someone has said that writers carry their homes, their identities, with them as expressed in their writings, and Alvarez has mapped out her own country, her own identity in her mind, one in which she is not Dominican or American, but a little of both.

In this text, we will read about losses, but in addition we will look at narratives for signposts that show the gains that come from becoming a "hyphenated," multicultural individual. In many ways we are all in process, changing as we go through life. With this can come rich opportunity. For Jill Ker Conway, leaving her native Australia to study at Harvard represented a beacon of hope and opportunity:

> *When the forms arrived, I was amused to discover that the applicant was asked to write a short biographical essay describing for the Admissions Committee the reasons why he or she had chosen to study history at Harvard. What would the hapless committee chairman do if I wrote the truth, I wondered? That I had come to an intellectual dead end in Australia; that I had rejected the cultural values of the country, and wanted an escape while there was still emotional life in me; that I needed to be somewhere where one could look at the history of empires truthfully; that life had been so trying recently that I had taken to drinking far too much, and hoped that life on a modest graduate student's stipend would help sober me up; that Cambridge was halfway round the world from Sydney, and that was a comfortable distance; that I was looking for a more congenial emotional environment, where ideas and feelings completed rather than denied one another (Conway, 1969, p. 234).*

Jill Ker Conway went on to graduate from Harvard and to be president of Smith College. She found a world that allowed her to develop her identity instead of repressing it due to an anti-feminist context in Australia and a dominating, controlling mother. She was enriched and given opportunity by crossing her border and writes about it in her autobiographic books *The Road from Coorain* and *True North*.

There is much to be learned by reading narratives of people who have crossed borders. In these we will look for signposts that indicate shifts in identity, and choices that were made that resulted in acculturation and self-determination. In addition, we will examine using ethnography as research to learn about identity. This knowledge can transfer to many occupations, especially teaching. We can create a learning environment that serves a diverse student population. Then, in the final section, we will look at ethnography as a tool for narrative research, as well as ways to learn to write ethnographies to learn about identity, adaptation, and acculturation, particularly in a classroom setting.

Questions for Discussion and Writing

1. What are the effects of moving from one place to another as discussed in the preceding examples? Give examples of negative and positive results.
2. Can you think of any other ways that identity shifts can occur from border crossing?
3. How can learning about identity help us create a learning environment for a diverse population of students?

CHAPTER 4

Poetry, Voice, and Identity

We have just examined how much we can learn from narrative, and we will continue our exploration in Chapter 5. Now, let us turn to poetry that illustrates voice and identity. Stories can be seen in all genres of literature, including poetry. The following poems are evocative of issues that form identity, and yet, at the same time, you don't have to know that much about the writer to get the sense of longing and of ennui. Sometimes the feeling reflects a collective consciousness, as in Derek Walcott's "A Far Cry from Africa." It can also evoke humor as in Andrei Codrescu's poem. Even the American poet Robert Frost captures the ambiguity in making choices that border-crossing individuals have to make. Other poems are more directly revealing as to the issues of identity.

Look at the following poem by Barbara Tran, a Vietnamese poet, to see her story as revealed in her poem.

Love and Rice

He jumped off the water buffalo, and I knew we'd be married.

He turned it easily pushing its head to the side.

The orange diep trees were like blazes of sun

hanging in the air below the clouds.

I told Mother that night he was my lover

He knew nothing of it.

I thought of nothing else as I wrung the sheets.

That he was my cousin didn't matter,

There was no room for shame.

Grandmother would notice the sun setting

and know her clock needed winding,

know she had missed her bananas and rice.

That first time I touched him, I thought of nothing but fruit.

There was no electricity then, night came early.

I took a long bath, pouring water

gently over my body, watching it drip

between the wooden slats.

Soon, I'd be carrying

a weight inside me. (2002)

Using your own words, tell the story of the person in the poem. Then, express the implied meaning. What changes are implied in the story? Now, read the following poem by Cathy Song called "*Lost Sister,*" and compare it with the identity of the person evoked in the previous poem.

Lost Sister

In China,

Even the peasants

Named their first daughters

Jade—

The stone that in the far fields

Could moisten the dry season,

Could make men move mountains

For the healing green of the inner hills

Glistening like slices of winter melon.

And the daughters were grateful:

They never left home.

To move freely was a luxury

Stolen from them at birth.

Instead, they gathered patience,

Learning to walk in shoes

The size of teacups,

Without breaking—

The arc of their movements

As dormant as the rooted willow,

As redundant as the farmyard hens.

But they traveled far

in surviving,

learning to stretch the family rice,

to quiet the demons,

the noisy stomachs.

There is a sister

Across the ocean,

Who relinquished her name,

Diluting jade green

With the blue of the Pacific.

Rising with a tide of locusts,

She swarmed with others

to inundate another shore.

In America,

there are many roads

and women can stride along with men.

But in another wilderness,

the possibilities,

the loneliness,

can strangulate like jungle vines.

The meager provisions and sentiments

of once belonging—

fermented roots, Mah-Jongg tiles and firecrackers—

set but a flimsy household

in a forest of nightless cities.

A giant snake rattles above,

Spewing black clouds into your kitchen.

Dough-faced landlords

slip in and out of your keyholes,

making claims you don't understand,

tapping into your communication systems

of laundry lines and restaurant chains.

You find you need China:

your one fragile identification,

A jade link

handcuffed to your wrist.

You remember your mother,

Who walked for centuries,

Footless—

And like her

you have left no footprints,

but only because

there is an ocean in between,

the unremitting space of your rebellion.

Activity. *Write a summary of the meaning of "Lost Sister." Compare it with the meaning of the previous poem by Barbara Tran.*

Here is a poem by Aurora Levin Morales that is evocative of the psychology of living in a hyphenated world in which boundaries are not clearly defined but sensed in the consciousness.

Child of the Americas

I am a child of the Americas,

A light-skinned mestiza of the Caribbean,

A child of many diaspora, born into this continent at a crossroads.

I am a U.S. Puerto Rican Jew

A product of the ghettos of New York I have never known.

An immigrant and the daughter and granddaughter of immigrants.

I speak English with passion: it's the tongue of my consciousness.

A flashing knife blade of crystal, my tool, my craft.

I am Caribena, island grown. Spanish is in my flesh,

Ripples from my tongue, lodges in my hips:

The language of garlic and mangoes,

The singing in my poetry, the flying gestures of my hands.

I am of Latinoamerica, rooted in the history of my continent:

I speak from that body.

I am not African. Africa is in me, but I cannot return.

I am not taina. Taino is in me, but there is no way back.

I am not European. Europe lives in me, but I have no home there.

I am new. History made me. My first language was Spanglish.

I was born at the crossroads

And I am whole.

Activity. *Analyze the use of language in Morales' poem to describe identity and sense of one's personal heritage.*

This next poem by Pat Mora shows the two worlds that exist in a person, one in the past and another in the present, and the part language plays in them.

Elena

My Spanish isn't enough

I remember how I'd smile

Listening to my little ones,

Understanding every word they say,

Their jokes, their songs, their plots.

Vamos a pedirle dulces a mama. Vamos.

But that was in Mexico.

Now my children go to American high schools.

They speak English. At night they sit around

The kitchen table, laugh with one another.

I stand by the stove and feel dumb, alone.

I bought a book to learn English.

My husband frowned, drank more beer.

My oldest said, Mama, he doesn't want you

To be smarter than he is: I'm forty

Embarrassed at mispronouncing words,

Embarrassed at the laughter of my children,

The grocer, the mailman. Sometimes I take

My English book and lock myself in the bathroom

Say the thick words softly,

For if I stop trying, I will be deaf

When my children need my help.

Activity. *Compare the two worlds Mora describes in her poem.*

Here, Gloria Anzaldúa, from her collection *Borderlands/La Frontera: The New Mestiza* (1987), describes a physical and psychological borderland.

To Live in the Borderlands Means You

To live in the Borderlands means you

   are neither hispana india negra española

   ni gabacha, eres mestiza, mulata, half-breed

   caught in the crossfire between camps

   while carrying all five races on your back

   not knowing which side to turn to, run from;

To live in the borderlands means knowing

   that the India *in you, betrayed for 500 years,*

   is no longer speaking to you,

   that mexicanas *call you* rajetas

   that denying the Anglo inside you

   is as bad as having denied the Indian or Black;

Cuando vives in la frontera

   people walk through you, the wind steals your voice,

   you're a burra, buey, *scapegoat,*

   forerunner of a new race,

   half and half—both woman and man, neither—

   a new gender;

To live in the Borderlands means to

   put chile *in the borscht*

   eat whole wheat tortillas,

   speak Tex-Mex with a Brooklyn accent;

   be stopped by la migra *at the border checkpoints;*

Living in the Borderlands means you fight hard to

   resist the gold elixir beckoning from the bottle,

   the pull of the gun barrel,

   the rope crushing the hollow of your throat;

In the Borderlands

   you are the battleground

   where enemies are kin to each other;

   you are at home, a stranger,

   the border disputes have been settled

   the volley of shots have shattered the truce

   you are wounded, lost in action

   dead, fighting back;

To live in the Borderlands means

   the mill with the razor white teeth wants to shred off

   your olive-red skin, crush out the kernel, your heart

   pound you pinch you roll you out

   smelling like white bread but dead;

To survive the borderlands

   you must live sin fronteras

   be a crossroads.

Activity. *What truths about identity does Anzaldúa explore? Read aloud the lines that illustrate these truths.*

Joseph Bruchas III wrote a poem that reflects his Slovak and Native American heritage.

Ellis Island

Beyond the red brick of Ellis Island

where the two Slovak children

who became my gradparents

waited the long days of quarantine;

after leaving the sickness,

the old Empires of Europe,

a Circle Line ship to the island slips easily

on its way to the island

of the tall woman, green

as dreams of forests and meadows

waiting for those who'd work

a thousand years

yet never owned their own.

Like millions of others,

I too come to this island,

nine decades the answerer

of dreams.

Yet only one part of my blood loves that memory.

Another voice speaks

of native lands

within this nation.

Lands invaded

when the earth became owned.

Lands of those who followed

the changing moon,

knowledge of the seasons

in their veins.

Activity. *Compare the two preceding poems, listing their differences in content and form.*

Note how this poem by Leslie Marmon Silko, also a Native American, reflects the poet's identity. As you read, notice the layout of the poem and consider how it affects your visual perception of meaning.

Where Mountain Lion Lay Down with Deer

I climb the black rock mountain

      Stepping from day to day

           Silently

I smell the wind for my ancestors

        Pale blue leaves

        Crushed wild mountain smell.

Returning

      Up the gray stone cliff

    Where I descended

        A thousand years ago.

Returning to faded black stone.

      Where mountain lion lay down with deer.

It is better to stay up here

           Watching wind's reflection

           In tall yellow flowers.

The old ones who remember me are gone

        The old songs are all forgotten

And the story of my birth.

How I danced in snow-frost moonlight

    Distant stars to the end of the Earth,

How I swam away

        In freezing mountain water

        Narrow mossy canyon tumbling down

           Out of the mountain

              Out of the deep canyon stone

      Down

        The memory

          Spilling out

          Into the world.

Activity. *Is the author of the poem speaking of herself or of her people? Sometimes identity in poetry is inferred indirectly, by metaphor. What is the poet saying about her sense of identity?*

Here is a poem by Chilean Nobel Prize–winner Pablo Neruda. What is he saying with regard to identity and going home? If you know Spanish, read the Spanish original version and see how the poem seems to differ in the two languages.

I Will Come Back

Sometime, man or woman,

traveler,

afterwards, when I am

not alive,

look here, look for me here

between the stones and

the ocean,

in the light storming

in the foam.

Look here, look for me here,

for here is where I shall come

saying nothing

no voice, no mouth, pure

here I shall be again the movement

of the water, of its

wild heart,

here I shall be both lost and found

here I shall be perhaps

both stone and silence.

Yo Volveré

Alguna vez, hombre o

mujer, viajero,

después, cuando no viva,

aquí buscad, buscadme

entre piedra y oceano

a la luz porcelaría

de la espuma

Aquí buscad, buscadme sin

decir nada porque aquí volveré sin

decir nada

sin voz, sin boca, puro

Aquí volveré a ser el movimiento

del agua, de su corazón, salvaje

aquí estaré perdido y encontrado

aquí seré a la vez piedra y silencia.

Activity. *Discuss the three preceding poems in tone and feeling. How are they similar and what is the longing expressed by the poet? How does it relate to our topic of story and context? What story is being told here?*

Now, let's examine a poem by 1992 Nobel Prize–winner Derek Walcott, the West Indian writer whose poetry connects Latin America's "magic realism" with myth and culture. See how different his voice is from the poem by Neruda. What similarities are there? If history is a story, what story is Walcott telling?

A Far Cry from Africa

A wind is ruffling the tawny pelt

Of Africa. Kikuyu, quick as flied

Batten upon the bloodstreams of the veldt.

Corpses are scattered through a paradise.

Only the worm, colonel of carrion, cries:

"Waste no compassion on these separate dead!"

Statistics justify and scholars seize

The salients of colonial policy.

What is that of the white child hacked in bed?

To savages, expendable as Jews?

Threshed out by beaters, the long ruses break

In a white dust of ibises whose cries

Have whelled since civilization's dawn

From the parched river or beast-teeming plain.

The violence of beast on beast is read

As natural law, but upright man

Seeks his divinity inflicting pain.

Delirious as these worried beasts, his wars

Dance to the tightened carcass of a drum,

While he calls courage still that native dread

Of the white peace contracted by the dead.

Again brutish necessity wipes its hands

Upon the napkin of a dirty cause again

A waste of our compassion, as with Spain,

The gorilla wrestles with the superman.

I who am poisoned with the blood of both,

Where shall I turn, divided to the vein?

I who have cursed

The drunken officer of British rule, how choose

Between this Africa and the English tongue I love?

Betray them both, or give back what they give?

How can I face such slaughter and be cool?

How can I turn from Africa and live?

Activity. *What conflicts does Walcott voice here? What history lesson are we learning here? What story? How often is history a story we can learn from? What generalizations can we draw from these two preceding poems?*

Read this classic poem by Robert Frost (1874–1963). How does it relate to the other poems in this chapter? You may already know this poem, but rereading it in this context may offer new insight.

The Road Not Taken

Two roads diverged in a yellow wood,

And sorry I could not travel both

And be one traveler, long I stood

And looked down one as far as I could

To where it bent in the undergrowth;

Then took the other, as just as fair,

And having perhaps the better claim,

Because it was grassy and wanted wear;

Though as for that the passing there

Had worn them really about the same,

And both that morning equally lay

In leaves no step had trodden black.

Oh, I kept the first for another day!

Yet knowing how way leads on to way,

I doubted if I should ever come back.

I shall be telling this with a sigh

Somewhere ages and ages hence:

Two roads diverged in a wood, and I—

I took the one less traveled by,

And that has made all the difference.

(1915)

Activity. *There is a great deal of controversy as to what Frost means in this poem. Did he choose well or badly? What do you think? What part of the poem made you decide? Now look back over the poems in this section and define the crossroads in each.*

The Romanian-born poet Andrei Codrescu, who now calls America his adopted home, writes about coming to America in this poem:

To the Western World

How I got to America

For Kris, who really knows

I swam over a barbed wire fence

There was a hair curtain and I scaled it

Then we closed the window

A rabbi hid me in his black skirt

A priest lent me a cassock

I dressed in a cow skin and munched

near the border

When the bull came I ran like hell

They traded me for a couple of spies.

I got a pass key to the western world

I made a fake ceiling on the Bucharest-Vienna pass

and curled in there with two of my best friends

and a bar of chocolate. The train went to Athens

instead and we died.

I wrote a letter to the President of America

and he sent Jimmy Carter to get me

with a diplomatic pouch just big enough

if I curled up real tight

There was a little war in the

Southern Carpathians

and some of us were catapulted into Yugoslavia

I married an extremely rich traveler

looking for her roots in my neighborhood

at about 10 P.M. on January, 1965.

I got inside the transistor radio and surfed

the Voice of America to Detroit

I wrapped my hand around the handle

of my broom and said the magic words;

Take me to the highs and save me from the lows!

But how I really got to America

only Kris really knows.

Activity. *What do you think the poem means with regard to identity and change?*

Activity for Discussion and Writing

Now write your own poem about your sense of identity and self.

Reread the preceding poems. Let your mind wander and roam. Write whatever comes to your mind in the form of poetry. Don't worry about the form. It can take the form of a prose-poem or Haiku. It can even be lyrics to a song. If you are artistically inclined, you can illustrate it. Then, if you wish, share it with your peers. Read it aloud, or ask someone to read it to you. What have you learned about identity and poetry?

CHAPTER 5

Fiction and the Self

When we read fiction written by writers who come from other cultures and who have other identities, we learn much about the divided self, the exiled identity, and the choices that the protagonists in the stories make. The choices determine the direction lives will take. Sometimes the choices are culturally or socially driven and come from the subconscious mind. Some are the result of loss and adaptation to the new home. We know that there are many factors that guide the acculturation process, as explored in *Lives in Two Languages*. However, it is when a sense of agency exists in the mind of the individual, a sense of acting on one's own as part of the process of writing one's own story, that an important aspect of gaining identity and controlling one's destiny occurs, as author Jill Kerr Conway wrote in *When Memory Speaks* (1999). As each person's narrative unfolds, markers as to choices made are revealed to the self. Each person composes his or her life, and a direction is taken from which consequences ensue, much like Robert Frost's "The Road Not Taken" describes in Chapter 4. The following excerpts from novels and memoirs were selected because they refer to a time when the individual made a decision that directly influenced a step in his or her unfolding identity. Although only excerpts are used in this book, for obvious reasons, I encourage students to read the complete novels and memoirs when possible or as homework.

White Teeth by Zadie Smith

In her acclaimed 2000 novel, *White Teeth*, Zadie Smith focuses on the clash in her native England over immigration, culture, and class. She also explores ways in which older generations realize their identities in contrast with the younger ones, a theme that also was explored in *Lives in Two Languages* (University of Michigan Press, 2001).

Like the writer herself, the protagonist, Irie, is half white and half Jamaican. She is a teenager growing up in London in the '90s. But she is not happy with her identity as revealed in her body image, especially her hair. Irie, which means "OK," decides to try to find a way to change everything about herself that reminds her of her past and Jamaican heritage. She wants to be considered "normal" by her teenage London schoolmates, and she especially wants to attract the attention of Millat, a second-generation Indian boy who likes to date slim, fair, straight-haired English girls. She decides to change her long, curly, Afro-style hair into long straight locks. The search for a sense of acceptable body image is a universal one with teenagers, but for immigrant teens like Irie, the sense of anxiety is intensified. Set in London in the 1990s, the excerpted passage illustrates her inner turmoil in the beauty parlor. We can tell that it is at the heart of her search for identity. She makes a choice and pays the consequence.

From *White Teeth* by Zadie Smith

The cryptically named P. K.'s Afro Hair: Design and Management sat between Fairweather Funeral Parlor and Raakshan Dentists, the convenient proximity meaning it was not at all uncommon for a cadaver of African origin to pass through all three establishments on his or her final journey to an open casket. So when you phoned for a hair appointment, and Andrea or Denise or Jackie told you *three-thirty Jamaican time,* naturally it meant come late, but there was also a chance it meant that some stone-cold churchgoing lady was determined to go to her grave with long fake nails and a weave-on. Strange as it sounds, there are plenty of people who refuse to meet the Lord with an Afro.

Irie, ignorant of all this, turned up for her appointment three-thirty on the dot, intent upon transformation, intent upon fighting her genes, a headscarf disguising the bird's nest of her hair, her right hand carefully placed upon her stomach.

"You wan' some ting, pickney?"

Straight hair. Straight straight long black sleek flickable tossable shakable touchable finger-through-able wind-blowable hair. With bangs.

"Three-thirty," was all Irie managed to convey of this, "with Andrea."

"Andrea's next door," replied the woman, pulling at a piece of elongated gum and nodding in the direction of Fairweather's, "having fun with the dearly departed. You better come sit down and wait and don' bodder me. Don't know how long she'll be."

Irie looked lost, standing in the middle of the shop, clutching her chub. The woman took pity, swallowed her gum, and looked Irie up and down; she felt more sympathetic as she noted Irie's cocoa complexion, the light eyes.

"Jackie."

"Irie."

"Pale, sir! Freckles an' every ting. You Mexican?"

"No."

"Arab?"

"Half Jamaican. Half English."

"Half-*caste*," Jackie explained patiently. "Your mum white?"

"Dad."

Jackie wrinkled her nose. "Usually de udder way roun'. How curly is it? Lemme see what's under dere—" She made a grab for Irie's headscarf. Irie, horrified at the possibility of being laid bare in a room full of people who got there before her and held on tight.

Jackie sucked her teeth. "What d'you 'spec us to do wid it if we kyant see it?"

Irie shrugged. Jackie shook her head amused.

"You ain't been in before?"

"No, never."

"What is it you want?"

"Straight," said Irie firmly, thinking of Nikki Tyler. "Straight and dark red."

"Is dat a fact! You wash your hair recent?"

"Yesterday," said Irie, offended. Jackie slapped her upside her head.

"Don' wash it! If you wan' it straight, don' wash it! You ever have ammonia on your head? It's like the devil's having a party on your scalp. You crazy? Don' wash it for two weeks an' den come back."

But Irie didn't have two weeks. She had it all planned; she was going to go round to Milat's this very evening with her new mane, all tied up in a bun, and she was going to take off her glasses and shake down her hair and he was going to say *why Miss Jones, I never would have supposed . . . why Miss Jones, you're—*

"I have to do it *today*. My sister's getting married."

"Well, when Andrea get back she going to burn seven shade of shit out of your hair an' you'll be luck if you don' walk out of here with a ball 'ed. But den it *your* funeral. Ear," she said, thrusting a pile of magazines into Irie's hands. "Dere," she said, pointing to a chair.

P. K.'s was split into two halves, male and female. In the male section, as relentless Ragga came unevenly over a battered stereo, young boys had logos cut into the backs of their heads at the hands of slightly older boys, skillful wielders of the electric trimmers. ADIDAS. BADMUTHA. MARTIN. The male section was all laughter, all talk all play; there was an easiness that sprang from no male haircut ever costing over six pounds or taking more than fifteen minutes. It was a simple-enough exchange and there was joy in it: the buzz of the revolving blade by your ear, a rough brush-down with a warm hand, mirrors front and back to admire the transformation. You came in with a picky head, uneven and coarse, disguised underneath a baseball cap, and you left swiftly afterward a new man, smelling sweetly of coconut oil and with a cut as sharp and clean as a swearword.

In comparison, the female section of P. K.'s was a deathly thing. Here, the impossible desire for straightness and "movement" fought daily with the stubborn determination of the curved African follicle; here ammonia, hot combs, clips, pins, and simple fire had all been enlisted in the war and were doing their damnedest to beat each curly hair into submission.

"Is it straight?" was the only question you heard as the towels came off and the heads emerged from the dryer pulsating with pain. "Is it straight, Denise? Tell me is it straight, Jackie?"

To which Jackie or Denise, having none of the obligations of white hairdressers, no need to make tea or kiss arse, flatter or make conversation (for these were not customers they were dealing with but desperate wretched *patients*), would give a skeptical snort and whip off the puke-green gown. "It as straight as it ever going to be!"

Four women sat in front of Irie now, biting their lips, staring intently into a long, dirty mirror, waiting for their straighter selves to materialize. While Irie flicked nervously through American black hair magazines, the four women sat grimacing in pain. Occasionally one said to another, "How long?" To which the proud reply came, "Fifteen minutes. How long for you?" "Twenty-two. This shit's been on my head twenty-two minutes. It *better* be straight."

It was a competition in agony. Like rich women in posh restaurants ordering ever-smaller salads.

Finally there would come a scream, or a "That's it! Shit, I can't take it!" and the head in question was rushed to the sink, where the washing could never be quick enough (you cannot get ammonia out of your hair quick enough) and the quiet weeping began. It was at this point that animosity arose; some people's hair was "kinkier" than others', some Afros fought harder, some survived. And the animosity spread from fellow customer to hairdresser, to inflicter of this pain, for it was natural enough to suspect Jackie or Denise of something like sadism: their fingers were too slow as they worked the stuff out, the water seemed to trickle instead of gush, and meanwhile the devil had a high old time burning the crap out of your hairline.

"Is it straight? Jackie, is it straight?"

The boys arched their heads round the partition wall, Irie looked up from her magazine. There was little to say. They all came out straight or straight enough. But they also came out dead. Dry. Splintered. Stiff. All the spring gone. Like the hair of a cadaver as the moisture seeps away.

Jackie or Denise, knowing full well that the curved African follicle will, in the end, follow its genetic instructions, put a philosophic slant on the bad news. "It as straight as it ever going to be. Tree weeks if you lucky."

Despite the obvious failure of the project, each woman along the line felt that it would be different for her, that when their own unveiling came, straight straight flickable, wind-blowable locks would be theirs. Irie, as full of confidence as the rest, returned to her magazine.

Malika, vibrant young star of the smash hit sitcom Malika's Life, explains how she achieves her loose and flowing look: "I hot wrap it each evening, ensuring that the ends are lightly waxed in African Queen Afro Sheen™, then, in the morning, I put a comb on the stove for approximately—"

The return of Andrea. The magazine was snatched from her hands, her headscarf unceremoniously removed before she could stop it, and five long and eloquent fingernails began to work their way over her scalp.

"Ooooh," murmured Andrea.

This sign of approval was a rare-enough occurrence for the rest of the shop to come round the partition to have a look.

"Oooooh," said Denise, adding her fingers to Andrea's. "So loose."

An older lady, wincing with pain underneath a dryer, nodded admiringly.

"Such a loose curl," cooed Jackie, ignoring her own scalded patient to reach into Irie's wool. "That's half-caste hair for you. I wish mine were like that. That'll relax beautiful."

Irie screwed up her face. "I *hate* it."

"She hates it!" said Denise to the crowd. "It's light brown in places!"

"I been dealing with a corpse all morning. Be nice to get my hands into somefing sof'," said Andrea, emerging from her reverie. "You gonna relax it, darlin'?"

"Yes. Straight. Straight and red."

Andrea tied a green gown round Irie's neck and lowered her into a swiveling chair. "Don't know about red, baby. Can't dye and relax on the same day. Kill the hair dead. But I can do the relax for you, no problem. Should come out beautiful, darlin'."

The communication between hairdressers in P. K.'s being poor, no one told Andrea that Irie had washed her hair. Two minutes after having the thick white ammonia gloop spread on to her head, she felt the initial cold sensation change to a terrific fire. There was no dirt there to protect the scalp, and Irie started screaming.

"I jus' put it on! You want it straight, don't you? Stop making that noise!"

"But it hurts!"

"Life hurts," said Andrea scornfully, "beauty hurts."

Irie bit her tongue for another thirty seconds until blood appeared above her right ear. Then the poor girl blacked out.

She came to with her head over the sink, watching her hair, which was coming out in clumps, shimmy down the plughole.

"You should have told me," Andrea was grumbling. "You should have told me that you washed it. It's got to be dirty first. Now look."

Now look. Hair that had once come down to her mid-vertebrae was only a few inches from her head.

"See what you've done," continued Andrea, as Irie wept openly. "I'd like to know what Mr. Paul King is going to say about this. I better phone him and see if we can fix this up for you for free."

Mr. Paul King, the P. K. in question, owned the place. He was a big white guy in his mid-fifties, who had been an entrepreneur in the building trade until Black Wednesday and his wife's credit card excesses took away everything but some bricks and mortar. Looking for a new idea, he read in the lifestyle section of his breakfast paper that black women spend five times as much as white women on beauty products and nine times as much on their hair. Taking his wife, Shelia, as an archetypal white woman, Paul King began to salivate. A little more research in his local library uncovered a multimillion pound industry. Paul King then bought a disused butcher's on Willesden High Road, head-hunted Andrea from a Harlesden salon, and gave black hairdressing a shot. It was an instant success. He was amazed to discover that women on low income were indeed prepared to spend hundreds of pounds per month on their hair and yet more on nails and accessories. He was vaguely amused when Andrea first explained to him that physical pain was also part of the process. And the best part of it was there was no question of suing—they *expected* the burns. Perfect business.

"Go on, Andrea, love, give her a freebie," said Paul King, shouting on a brick-shaped mobile over the construction noise of his new salon, opening in Wembley. "But don't make a habit of it."

Andrea returned to Irie with the good tidings. "'Sal right, darlin'. His one's on us."

"But what—" Irie stared at her Hiroshima reflection. "What can you—"

"Put your scarf back on, turn left out of here, and go down the High Road until you get to a shop called Roshi's Haircare. Take this card and tell them P. K.'s sent you. Get eight packets of number-five-type black hair with a red glow and come back here quick style."

"Hair?" repeated Irie through snot and tears. "*Fake* hair?"

"Stupid girl. It's not fake. It's real. And when it's on your head, it'll be you real hair. Go!"

Blubbing like a baby, Irie shuffled out of P. K.'s and down the High Road, trying to avoid her reflection in the shop windows. Reaching Roshi's, she did her best to pull herself together, put her right hand over her stomach and pushed through the doors.

* * *

Questions for Discussion and Writing

1. There is an irony in the results of Irie's trip to the beauty parlor. What is it?

2. Zadie Smith has a wonderful ear for dialogue. Discuss how the Jamaican dialect at the beauty shop differs from Irie's speech. How would you deal with this dialect in the English as a second language class?

3. Irie tells the beautician that she is going to a wedding as the reason for getting her hair transformed immediately. What is the real reason?

4. Carol Gilligan (1992), a researcher and child psychologist from Harvard, says that teenage girls lose their sense of self-worth after puberty, and they need strong role models who are female to help them regain it. What ways would you try to give a teen like Irie self-esteem? What could you do in the classroom?

5. In the excerpt we get many clues that this solution to Irie's self-image problem is not going to work. What are these clues?

The Color of Water by James McBride

Like the texture of hair, the color of skin is central to identity. In James McBride's moving and complex memoir, he touches on many complex issues, such as race, religion, and identity. James, like Zadie Smith, writes from the point of view of a person who has a white parent—in this case, his mother, and an African-American father. While searching for the way to relieve an unsettling sense of "anomie," he came to realize that he needed to know more about the most interesting person he had ever known and the biggest influence on his identity—his mother, Ruth McBride Jordan, the daughter of a failed Jewish rabbi. Unlike Irie in *White Teeth* who wants to separate from her past and individuate, James comes to believe maternal love is central to making him a successful person. The excerpted passage describes his growing awareness that life was going to be problematic for him, but that the love and nurturing his mother gave him were huge assets in confronting these problems. McBride illustrates the points at which his perception of identity slowly changes as he learns about his mother. We can imagine the choices that will lie ahead.

From *The Color of Water* by James McBride

When I was a boy, I used to wonder where my mother came from, how she got on this earth. When I asked her where she was from, she would say, "God made me," and change the subject. When I asked her if she was white, she'd say, "No. I'm light-skinned," and change the subject again. Answering questions about her personal history did not jibe with Mommy's view of parenting twelve curious, wild, brown-skinned children. She issued orders and her rule was law. Since she refused to divulge details about herself or her past, and because my stepfather was largely unavailable to deal with questions about himself or Ma, what I learned of Mommy's past I learned from my siblings. We traded information on Mommy the way people trade baseball cards at trade shows, offering bits and pieces fraught with gossip, nonsense, wisdom, and sometimes just plain foolishness. "What does it matter to you?" my older brother Richie scoffed when I asked him if we had any grandparents. "You're adopted anyway."

My siblings and I spent hours playing tricks and teasing one another. It was a way of dealing with realities over which we had no control. I told Richie I didn't believe him.

"I don't care if you believe me or not," he sniffed. "Mommy's not your real mother. Your real mother's in jail."

"You're lying!"

"You'll see when Mommy takes you back to your real mother next week. Why do you think she's been so nice to you all week?"

Suddenly it occurred to me that Mommy *had* been nice to me all week. But wasn't she nice to me all the time? I couldn't remember, partly because within my confused eight-year-old reasoning was a growing fear that maybe Richie was right. Mommy, after all, did not really look like me. In fact, she didn't really look like Richie, or David—or any of her children for that matter. We were all clearly black, of various shades of brown, some light brown, some medium brown, some very light-skinned, and all of us had curly hair. Mommy was, by her own definition, "light-skinned," a statement which I had initially accepted as fact but at some point later decided was not true. My best friend Billy Smith's mother was as light as Mommy was and had red hair to boot, but there was no question in my mind that Billy's mother was black and my mother was not. There was something inside me, an ache I had, like a constant itch that got bigger and bigger as I grew, that told me. It was in my blood, you might say, and however the notion got there, it bothered me greatly. Yet Mommy refused to acknowledge her whiteness. Why she did so was not clear, but even my teachers seemed to know she was white and I wasn't. On open school nights, the question most often asked by my schoolteachers was: "Is James adopted?" which always prompted an outraged response from Mommy.

I told Richie: "If I'm adopted, you're adopted too."

"Nope," Richie replied. "Just you, and you're going back to your real mother in jail."

"I'll run away first."

"You can't do that. Mommy will get in trouble if you do that. You don't want to see Ma get in trouble, do you? It's not her fault that you're adopted, is it?"

He had me then. Panic set in. "But I don't want to go to my real mother. I want to stay here with Ma . . ."

"You gotta go. I'm sorry, man."

This went on until I was in tears. I remember pacing about nervously all day while Richie, knowing he had ruined my life, cackled himself to sleep. That night I lay wide awake in bed waiting for Mommy to get home from work at two A.M., whereupon she laid the ruse out as I sat at the kitchen table in my tattered Fruit of the Loom underwear. "You're not adopted," she laughed.

"So you're my real mother?"

"Of course I am." Big kiss.

"Then who's my grandparents?"

"Your grandpa Nash died and so did your grandma Etta."

"Who were they?"

"They were your father's parents."

"Where were they from?"

"From down south. You remember them?"

I had a faint recollection of my grandmother Etta, an ancient black woman with a beautiful face who seemed very confused, walking around with a blue dress and a fishing pole, the bait, tackle, and line dragging down around her ankles. She didn't seem real to me.

"Did you know them, Ma?"

"I knew them very, very well."

"Did they love you?"

"Why do you ask so many questions?"

"I just want to know. Did they love you? Because your own parents didn't love you, did they?"

"My own parents loved me."

"Then where are they?"

A short silence. "My mother died many, many years ago," she said. "My father, he was a fox. No more questions tonight. You want some coffee cake?" Enough said. If getting Mommy's undivided attention for more than five minutes was a great feat in a family of twelve kids, then getting a midnight snack in my house was a greater thrill. I cut the questions and ate the cake, though it never stopped me from wondering, partly because of fear for her safety, because even as a child I had a clear sense that black and white folks did not get along, which put her, and us, in a pretty tight space.

In 1966, when I was nine, black power had permeated every element of my neighborhood in St. Albans, Queens. Malcolm X had been killed the year before and had grown larger in death than in life. Afros were in style. The Black Panthers were a force. Public buildings, statues, monuments, even trees, met the evening in their original bland colors and reemerged the next morning painted in the sparkling "liberation colors" of red, black, and green. Congas played at night on the streets while teenyboppers gathered to talk of revolution. My siblings marched around the house reciting poetry from the Last Poets, a sort of rap group who recited in-your-face poetry with conga and fascinating vocal lines serving as a musical backdrop, with songs titled "Niggers Are Scared of Revolution" and "On the Subway." Every Saturday morning my friends and I would pedal our bicycles to the corner of Dunkirk Street and Ilion Avenue to watch the local drag racers near the Sun Dew soft drink factory, trying to see who could drive the fastest over a dip in the road that sent even the slowest-moving car airborne. My stepfather hit that dip at fifteen miles an hour in his '64 Pontiac and I bounced high in my seat. These guys hit it at ninety and their cars flew like birds, barreling through the air and landing fifteen feet away, often skidding out of control, sometimes smacking against the wall of the Sun Dew factory before wobbling away in a pile of bent metal, grilles, and fenders. Their cars had names like "Smokin' Joe" and "Miko" and "Dream Machine" scrawled on the hoods, but our favorite was a gleaming black, souped-up GTO with the words "Black Power" written in smooth white script across the hood and top. It was the fastest and its driver was, of course, the coolest. He drove like a madman, and after leaving some poor Corvette in the dust, he'd power his mighty car in a circle, wheel it around, and do a victory lap for us, driving at low speed, one muscled arm angling out the window, his car rumbling powerfully, while we whistled and cheered, raising our fists and yelling, "Black power!" He'd laugh and burn rubber for us, tires screeching, roaring away in a burst of gleaming metal and hot exhaust, his taillights flashing as he disappeared into the back alleyways before the cops had a chance to bust him. We thought he was God.

But there was a part of me that feared black power very deeply for the obvious reason. I thought black power would be the end of my mother. I had swallowed the white man's fear of the Negro, as we were called back then, whole. It began with a sober white newsman on our black-and-white television set introducing a news clip showing a Black Panther rally, led by Bobby Seale or Huey Newton or one of those young black militant leaders, screaming to hundreds and hundreds of angry African-American students, "Black power! Black power! Black power!" while the crowd roared. It frightened the shit out of me. I thought to myself, *These people will kill Mommy.* Mommy, on the other hand, seemed unconcerned. Her motto was, "If it doesn't involve your going to school or church, I could care less about it and my answer is no whatever it is."

She insisted on absolute privacy, excellent school grades, and trusted no outsiders of either race. We were instructed never to reveal details of our home life to any figures of authority: teachers, social workers, cops, storekeepers, or even friends. If anyone asked us about our home life, we were taught to respond with, "I don't know," and for years I did just that. Mommy's house was an entire world that she created. She appointed the eldest child at home to be "king" or "queen" to run the house in her absence and we took it from there, creating court jesters, slaves, musicians, poets, pets, and clowns. Playing in the street was discouraged and often forbidden and if you did manage to slip out, "Get your butt in this house before dark," she would warn, a rule she enforced to the bone. I often played that rule out to its very edge, stealing into the house at dusk, just as the last glimmer of sunlight was peeking over the western horizon, closing the door softly, hoping Mommy had gone to work, only to turn around and find her standing before me, hands on hips, whipping belt in hand, eyes flicking angrily back and forth to the window, then to me, lips pursed, trying to decide whether it was light or dark outside. "It's still light," I'd suggest, my voice wavering, as my siblings gathered behind her to watch the impending slaughter.

"That looks like light to you?" she'd snap, motioning to the window.

"Looks pretty dark," my siblings would chirp from behind her. "It's definitely dark, Ma!" they'd shout, stifling their giggles. If I was lucky a baby would wail in another room and she'd be off, hanging the belt on the doorknob as she went. "Don't do it again," she'd warn over her shoulder, and I was a free man.

But even if she had any interest in black power, she had no time to talk about it. She worked the swing shift at Chase Manhattan Bank as a typist, leaving home at three P.M. and returning around two A.M., so she had little time for games, and even less time for identity crises. She and my father brought a curious blend of Jewish-European and African-American distrust and paranoia into our house. On his end, my father, Andrew McBride, a Baptist minister, had his doubts about the world accepting his mixed family. He always made sure his kids never got into trouble, was concerned about money, and trusted the providence of the Holy Father to do the rest. After he died and Mommy remarried, my stepfather, Hunter Jordan, seemed to pick up where my father left off, insistent on education and church. On her end, Mommy had no model for raising us other than the experience of her own Orthodox Jewish family, which despite the seeming flaws—an unbending nature, a stridency, a focus on money, a deep distrust of all outsiders, not to mention her father's tyranny—represented the best and worst of the immigrant mentality: hard work, no nonsense, quest for excellence, distrust of authority figures, and a deep belief in God and education. My parents were nonmaterialistic. They believed that money without knowledge was worthless, that education tempered with religion was the way to climb out of poverty in America, and over the years they were proven right.

Yet conflict was a part of our lives, written into our very faces, hands, and arms, and to see how contradiction lived and survived in its essence, we had to look no farther than our own mother. Mommy's contradictions crashed and slammed against one another like bumper cars at Coney Island. White folks, she felt, were implicitly evil toward blacks, yet she forced us to go to white schools to get the best education. Blacks could be trusted more, but anything involving blacks was probably slightly substandard. She disliked people with money yet was in constant need of it. She couldn't stand racists of either color and had great distaste for bourgeois blacks who sought to emulate rich whites by putting on airs and "doing silly things like covering their couches with plastic and holding teacups with their pinkies out." "What fools!" she'd hiss. She wouldn't be bothered with parents who bragged about their children's accomplishments, yet she insisted we strive for the highest professional goals. She was against welfare and never applied for it despite our need, but championed those who availed themselves of it. She hated restaurants and would not enter one even if the meals served were free. She actually preferred to be among the poor, the working-class poor of the Red Hook Housing Projects in Brooklyn, the cement mixers, bakers, doughnut makers, grandmothers, and soul-food church partisans who were her lifelong friends. It was with them that she and my father started the New Brown Memorial Baptist Church, a small storefront church which still stands in Red Hook today. Mommy loves that church and to this day still loves Red Hook, one of the most dangerous and neglected housing projects in New York City. On any given day she'll get up in the morning, take the New Jersey Transit train from her home in Ewing, New Jersey, to Manhattan, then take the subway to Brooklyn, and wander around the projects like the Pope, the only white person in sight, waving to friends, stepping past the drug addicts, smiling at the young mothers pushing their children in baby carriages, slipping into the poorly lit hallway of 80 Dwight Street while the young dudes in hooded sweatshirts stare balefully at the strange, bowlegged old white lady in Nikes and red sweats who slowly hobbles up the three flights of dark, urine-smelling stairs on arthritic knees to visit her best friend, Mrs. Ingram in apartment 3G.

* * *

Questions for Discussion and Writing

1. Why do you think Ruth refused to acknowledge her whiteness, calling herself "light-skinned" at a time in the '60s when everyone was race-conscious? What does that fact suggest?
2. What fears did he have for his mother that kept him from embracing his African identity as expressed by the Black Panther movement?
3. In the brief excerpt of dialogue on p. 46, what more do we learn about Ruth's personality?
4. Why was McBride afraid of the Black Panther movement?
5. All of her 12 children grew up to be successful. From this brief excerpt, what parenting practices might have been partly responsible?
6. How do you think multiracial children with varying skin colors deal with being in a predominantly white school? Does this complicate the acculturation process?
7. In what ways do you think McBride's decision to write about his mother helped his identity evolve?
8. This excerpt takes place mostly in the '60s, whereas Irie's story in the preceding exerpt took place in the '90s. How does this difference affect the stories?

The Namesake by Jhumpa Lahiri

Thus far, we have dealt with body image and skin color as being central to a sense of identity. In Pulitzer Prize-winner Jhumpa Lahiri's novel *The Namesake*, the protagonist, Gogol Ganguli, struggles with the generation gap that is focused on the name his father gave him for a pet name. As in Bengali custom, he also has a given name, Nikhil. Gogol was given his name because his father was reading *The Overcoat* by the Russian novelist Nikolai Gogol during a terrible train wreck, and the book, he felt, had saved his life. In gratitude, Ashoke decides to name his son after his favorite author, an exile like himself. The unusual name, neither American nor Bengali, causes a problem for the young man. Not knowing why his father named him Gogol makes it even harder to bear the uneasiness. Of course, the name is merely part of a growing identity crisis. When he gets ready to go to college at Yale, he feels it will keep him from fitting in with his other classmates. In the following passage, Gogol decides to make a choice and change his name. In doing so, he is exercising the sense of identity that helps move him along toward his own destiny.

From *The Namesake* by Jhumpa Lahiri

Plenty of people changed their names: actors, writers, revolutionaries, transvestites. In history class, Gogol has learned that European immigrants had their names changed at Ellis Island, that slaves renamed themselves once they were emancipated. Though Gogol doesn't know it, even Nikolai Gogol renamed himself, simplifying his surname at the age of twenty-two from Gogol-Yanovsky to Gogol upon publication in the *Literary Gazette*. (He had also published under the name Yanov, and once signed his work "OOOO" in honor of the four *o*'s in his full name.)

One day in the summer of 1986, in the frantic weeks before moving away from his family, before his freshman year at Yale is about to begin, Gogol Ganguli does the same. He rides the commuter rail into Boston, switching to the Green Line at North Station, getting out at Lechmere. The area is somewhat familiar: he has been to Lechmere countless times with his family, to buy new televisions and vacuum cleaners, and he has been to the Museum of Science on field trips from school. But he has never been to this neighborhood on his own, and in spite of the directions he's written on a sheet of paper he gets briefly lost on his way to the Middlesex Probate and Family Court. He wears a blue oxford shirt, khakis, a camel-colored corduroy blazer bought for his college interviews that is too warm for the sultry day. Knotted around his neck is his only tie, maroon with yellow stripes on the diagonal. By now Gogol is just shy of six feet tall, his body slender, his thick brown-black hair slightly in need of a cut. His face is lean, intelligent, suddenly handsome, the bones more prominent, the pale gold skin clean-shaven and clear. He has inherited Ashima's* eyes, large, penetrating, with bold, elegant brows, and shares with Ashoke** the slight bump at the very top of his nose.

The courthouse is an imposing, old pillared brick building occupying a full city block, but the entrance is off to the side, down a set of steps. Inside, Gogol empties his pockets and steps through a metal detector, as if he were at an airport, about to embark on a journey. He is soothed by the chill of the air-conditioning, by the beautifully carved plaster ceiling, by the voices that echo pleasantly in the marbled interior. He had pictured a setting far less grand. And yet this is a place, he gathers, that people come to seek divorces, dispute wills. A man at the information booth tells him to wait upstairs, in an area filled with round tables, where people sit eating their lunch. Gogol sits impatiently, one long leg jiggling up and down. He has forgotten to bring a book to read and so he picks up a discarded section of the *Globe,* skimming an article in the "Arts" section about Andrew Wyeth's Helga paintings. Eventually he begins to practice his new signature in the margins of the paper. He tries it in various styles, his hand unaccustomed to the angles of the *N,* the dotting of the two *i*'s. He wonders how many times he has written his old name, at the tops of how many tests and quizzes, how many homework assignments, how many yearbook inscriptions to friends. How many times does a person write his name in a lifetime—a million? Two million?

The idea to change his name had first occurred to him a few months ago. He was sitting in the waiting room of his dentist, flipping through an issue of *Reader's Digest.* He'd been turning the pages at random until he came to an article that caused him to stop. The article was called "Second Baptisms." "Can you identify the following famous

---

*Ashima is Gogol's mother.
**Ashoke is Gogol's father.

people?" was written beneath the headline. A list of names followed and, at the bottom of the page, printed in tiny letters upside down, the famous personalities they corresponded to. The only one he guessed correctly was Robert Zimmerman, Bob Dylan's real name. He had no idea that Molière had been born Jean-Baptiste Poquelin and that Leon Trotsky was born Lev Davidovich Bronstein. That Gerald Ford's name was Leslie Lynch King, Jr., and that Engelbert Humperdinck's was Arnold George Dorsey. They had all renamed themselves, the article said, adding that it was a right belonging to every American citizen. He read that tens of thousands of Americans had their names changed each year. All it took was a legal petition, the article had said. And suddenly he envisioned "Gogol" added to the list of names, "Nikhil" printed in tiny letters upside down.

That night at the dinner table, he brought it up with his parents. It was one thing for Gogol to be the name penned in calligraphy on his high school diploma, and printed below his picture in the yearbook, he'd begun. It was one thing, even, for it to be typed on his applications to five Ivy League colleges, as well as to Stanford and Berkeley. But engraved, four years from now, on a bachelor of arts degree? Written at the top of a résumé? Centered on a business card? It would be the name his parents picked out for him, he assured them, the good name they'd chosen for him when he was five.

"What's done is done," his father had said. "It will be a hassle. Gogol has, in effect, become your good name."

"It's too complicated now," his mother said, agreeing. "You're too old."

"I'm not," he persisted. "I don't get it. Why did you have to give me a pet name in the first place? What's the point?"

"It's our way, Gogol," his mother maintained. "It's what Bengalis do."

"But it's not even a Bengali name."

He told his parents what he'd learned in Mr. Lawson's class, about Gogol's lifelong unhappiness, his mental instability, about how he'd starved himself to death. "Did you know all this stuff about him?" he asked.

"You forgot to mention that he was also a genius," his father said.

"I don't get it. How could you guys name me after someone so strange? No one takes me seriously," Gogol said.

"Who? Who does not take you seriously?" his father wanted to know, lifting his fingers from his plate, looking up at him.

"People," he said, lying to his parents. For his father had a point; the only person who tormented him, the only person chronically aware of and afflicted by the embarrassment of his name, the only person who constantly questioned it and wished it were otherwise, was Gogol. And yet he'd continued, saying that they should be glad, that his official name would be Bengali, not Russian.

"I don't know, Gogol," his mother had said, shaking her head. "I really don't know." She got up to clear the dishes. Sonia* slinked away, up to her room. Gogol remained at the table with his father. They sat there together, listening to his mother scraping the plates, the water running in the sink.

"Then change it," his father said simply, quietly, after a while.

"Really?"

"In America anything is possible. Do as you wish."

And so he had obtained a Commonwealth of Massachusetts change-of-name form, to submit along with a certified copy of his birth certificate and a check to the Middlesex Probate and Family Court. He'd brought the form to his father, who had glanced at it only briefly before signing his consent, with the same resignation with which he signed a check or credit card receipt, his eyebrows slightly raised over his glasses, inwardly calculating the loss. He'd filled out the rest of the form in his room, later at night when his family was asleep. The application consisted of a single side of a cream-colored sheet, and yet it had taken him longer to fill out than his applications for college. On the first line he filled out the name he wished to change, and his place and date of birth. He wrote in the new name he wished to adopt, then signed the form with his old signature. Only one part of the form had given him pause: in approximately three lines, he was asked to provide a reason for seeking the change. For nearly an hour he'd sat there, wondering what to write. He'd left it blank in the end.

At the appointed time, his case is called. He enters a room and sits on an empty wooden bench at the back. The judge, a middle-aged, heavyset black woman wearing half-moon glasses, sits opposite, on a dais. The clerk, a thin young woman with bobbed hair, asks for

*Sonia is Gogol's sister.

his application, reviewing it before handing it to the judge. There is nothing decorating the room apart from the Massachusetts state and American flags and an oil portrait of a judge. "Gogol Ganguli," the clerk says, motioning for Gogol to approach the dais, and as eager as he is to go through with it, he is aware, with a twinge of sadness, that this is the last time in his life he will hear that name uttered in an official context. In spite of his parents' sanction he feels that he is overstepping them, correcting a mistake they've made.

"What is the reason you wish to change your name, Mr. Ganguli?" the judge asks.

The question catches him off-guard, and for several seconds he has no idea what to say. "Personal reasons," he says eventually. The judge looks at him, leaning forward, her chin cupped in her hand. "Would you care to be more specific?"

At first he says nothing, unprepared to give any further explanation. He wonders whether to tell the judge the whole convoluted story, about his great-grandmother's letter that never made it to Cambridge, and about pet names and good names, about what had happened on the first day of kindergarten. But instead he takes a deep breath and tells the people in the courtroom what he has never dared admit to his parents. "I hate the name Gogol," he says. "I've always hated it."

"Very well," the judge says, stamping and signing the form, then returning it to the clerk. He is told that notice of the new name must be given to all other agencies, that it's his responsibility to notify the Registry of Motor Vehicles, banks, schools. He orders three certified copies of the name change decree, two for himself, and one for his parents to keep in their safe-deposit box. No one accompanies him on this legal rite of passage, and when he steps out of the room no one is waiting to commemorate the moment with flowers and Polaroid snapshots and balloons. In fact the procedure is entirely unmomentous, and when he looks at his watch, he sees that from the time he'd entered the courtroom it had taken all of ten minutes. He emerges into the muggy afternoon, perspiring, still partly convinced it was a dream. He takes the T across the river to Boston. He walks with his blazer clasped by a finger over his shoulder, across the Common, through the Public Garden, over the bridges and along the curving paths that rim the lagoon. Thick clouds conceal the sky, which appears only here and there like the small lakes on a map, and the air threatens rain.

He wonders if this is how it feels for an obese person to become thin, for a prisoner to walk free. "I'm Nikhil," he wants to tell the people who are walking their dogs, pushing children in their strollers, throwing bread to the ducks. He wanders up Newbury Street as drops begin to fall. He dashes into Newbury Comics, buys himself *London Calling* and *Talking Heads: 77* with his birthday money, a Che poster for his dorm room. He pockets an application for a student American Express card, grateful that his first credit card will not say Gogol in raised letters at the bottom. "I'm Nikhil," he is tempted to tell the attractive, nose-ringed cashier with dyed black hair and skin as pale as paper. The cashier hands him his change and looks past him to the next customer, but it doesn't matter; instead he thinks of how many more women he can now approach, for the rest of his life, with this same unobjectionable, uninteresting fact. Still, for the next three weeks, even though his new driver's license says "Nikhil," even though he's sliced up the old one with his mother's sewing scissors, even though he's ripped out the pages in front of his favorite books in which he'd written his name until now, there's a snag: everyone he knows in the world still calls him Gogol. He is aware that his parents, and their friends, and the children of their friends, and all his own friends from high school, will never call him anything but Gogol. He will remain Gogol during holidays and in summer; Gogol will revisit him on each of his birthdays. Everyone who comes to his going-away-to-college party writes "Good Luck, Gogol" on the cards.

It isn't until his first day in New Haven, after his father and teary mother and Sonia are heading back up 95 toward Boston, that he begins to introduce himself as Nikhil. The first people to call him by his new name are his suitemates, Brandon and Jonathan, both of whom had been notified by mail over the summer that his name is Gogol. Brandon, lanky and blond, grew up in Massachusetts not far from Gogol, and went to Andover. Jonathan, who is Korean and plays the cello, comes from L.A.

"Is Gogol your first name or your last?" Brandon wants to know.

Normally that question agitates him. But today he has a new answer. "Actually, that's my middle name," Gogol says by way of explanation, sitting with them in the common room to their suite. "Nikhil is my first name. It got left out for some reason."

Jonathan nods in acceptance, distracted by the task of setting up his stereo components. Brandon nods, too. "Hey, Nikhil," Brandon says awhile later, after they have arranged the furniture in the common room to their liking. "Want to smoke a bowl?" Since everything else is suddenly so new, going by a new name doesn't feel so terribly strange to Gogol. He lives in a new state, has a new telephone number. He eats his meals off a tray in Commons, shares a bathroom with a floor full of people, showers each morning in a stall. He sleeps in a new bed, which his mother had insisted on making before she left.

He spends the days of orientation rushing around campus, back and forth along the intersecting flagstone path, past the clock tower, and the turreted, crenellated buildings. He is too harried, at first, to sit on the grass in Old Campus as the other students do, perusing their course catalogues, playing Frisbee, getting to know one another among the verdigris-covered statues of robed, seated men. He makes a list of all the places he has to go, circling the buildings on his campus map. When he is alone in his room he types out a written request on his Smith Corona, notifying the registrar's office of his name change, proving examples of his former and current signatures side by side. He gives these documents to a secretary, along with a copy of the change-of-name form. He tells his freshman counselor about his name change; he tells the person in charge of processing his student ID and his library card. He corrects the error in stealth, not bothering to explain to Jonathan and Brandon what he's so busy doing all day, and then suddenly it is over. After so much work it is no work at all. By the time the upperclassmen arrive and classes begin, he's paved the way for a whole university to call him Nikhil: students and professors and TAs and girls at parties. Nikhil registers for his first four classes: Intro to the History of Art, Medieval History, a semester of Spanish, Astronomy to fulfill his hard science requirement. At the last minute he registers for a drawing class in the evenings. He doesn't tell his parents about the drawing class, something they would consider frivolous at this stage of his life, in spite of the fact that his own grandfather was an artist. They are already distressed that he hasn't settled on a major and a profession. Like the rest of their Bengali friends, his parents expect him to be, if not an engineer, an economist at the very least. These were the fields that brought them to America, his father repeatedly reminds him, the professions that have earned them security and respect.

But now that he's Nikhil it's easier to ignore his parents, to tune out their concerns and pleas. With relief, he types his name at the tops of his freshman papers. He reads the telephone messages his suitemates leave for Nikhil on assorted scraps in their rooms. He opens up a checking account, writes his new name into course books. *"Me llamo Nikhil,"* he says in his Spanish class. It is as Nikhil, that first semester, that he grows a goatee, starts smoking Camel Lights at parties and while writing papers and before exams, discovers Brian Eno and Elvis Costello and Charlie Parker. It is as Nikhil that he takes Metro-North into Manhattan one weekend with Jonathan and gets himself a fake ID that allows him to be served liquor in New Haven bars. It is as Nikhil that he loses his virginity at a party at Ezra Stiles, with a girl wearing a plaid woolen skirt and combat boots and mustard tights. By the time he wakes up, hung-over, at three in the morning, she has vanished from the room, and he is unable to recall her name.

There is only one complication: he doesn't feel like Nikhil. Not yet. Part of the problem is that the people who now know him as Nikhil have no idea that he used to be Gogol. They know him only in the present not at all in the past. But after eighteen years of Gogol, two months of Nikhil feel scant, inconsequential. At times he feels as if he's cast himself in a play, acting the part of twins, indistinguishable to the naked eye yet fundamentally different. At times he still feels his old name, painfully and without warning, the way his front tooth had unbearably throbbed in recent weeks after a filling, threatening for an instant to sever from his gums when he drank coffee, or iced water, and once when he was riding in an elevator. He fears being discovered, having the whole charade somehow unravel, and in nightmares his files are exposed, his original name printed on the front page of the *Yale Daily News*. Once, he signs his old name by mistake on a credit card slip at the college bookstore. Occasionally he has to hear Nikhil three times before he answers.

Even more startling is when those who normally call him Gogol refer to him as Nikhil. For example, when his parents call on Saturday mornings, if Brandon or Jonathan happens to pick up the phone, they ask if Nikhil is there. Though he has asked his parents to do precisely this, the act of it troubles him, making him feel in that instant that he is not related to them, not their child. "Please come to our home with Nikhil one weekend," Ashima says to his roommates when she and Ashoke visit campus during parents weekend in October, the suite hastily cleared of liquor bottles and ashtrays and Brandon's bong for the occasion. The substitution sounds wrong to Gogol, correct but off-key, the way it sounds when his parents speak English to him instead of Bengali. Stranger still is when one of his parents addresses him, in front of his new friends, as Nikhil directly: "Nikhil, show us the buildings where you have your classes," his father suggests. Later that evening, out to dinner with Jonathan at a restaurant on Chapel Street, Ashima slips, asking, "Gogol, have you decided yet what your major will be?" Though Jonathan, listening to something his father is saying, doesn't hear, Gogol feels helpless, annoyed yet unable to blame his mother, caught in the mess he's made.

* * *

Questions for Discussion and Writing

1. Describe the journey Gogol takes when he goes to get his name changed.
2. In what ways is changing his name part of the process of individuation, separating from one's parents?
3. What are the cultural attitudes toward names and naming in Gogol's family that vary from your own?
4. What is the difference between a pet name and a good name in Bengali culture?
5. Why does Gogol feel sad when he is finally called by the judge to change his name? Then, later, he finds he doesn't feel like Nikhil; why do you think this happens?
4. What is your prediction as to how this choice will affect his relationship with his family and native culture?
5. Of the three characteristics of identity—skin, hair texture, and name—which ones are hardest to change?
6. In second language classrooms, what precautions do you make to be sensitive to how a child may feel about his or her name?

Half a Life by V.S. Naipul

In the graceful prose for which he has become famous, V.S. Naipul examines what it is like to search for an identity in a "half-life" existence. In a narrative that spans three continents and several decades, the writer focuses on one young man, Willie Chandron, whose life takes many twists and turns as he travels from the Caribbean to London and to Africa where he attempts becoming a writer. After searching for meaning in his life in London's West End society, he finally meets a girl named Ana. In the excerpted passage, the decision to marry Ana and move to Africa makes his life take a long direction that he would not have dreamed of as a rebellious youth. He is now in a totally unfamiliar world, and he tries to find the contentment that eluded him in London. Here, he is writing about his life in Africa to his sister Sarojini who still lives in Europe.

From *Half a Life* by V.S. Naipul

The first day at Ana's estate house (Willie said) was as long as you can imagine. Everything in the house—the colours, the wood, the furniture, the smells—was new to me. Everything in the bathroom was new to me—all the slightly antiquated fittings, and the old geyser for heating water. Other people had designed that room, had had those fittings installed, had chosen those white wall tiles—some of them cracked now, the crack-lines and the grouting black with mould or dirt, the walls themselves a little uneven. Other people had become familiar with all those things, had considered them part of the comfort of the house. In that room especially I felt a stranger.

Somehow I got through the day, without Ana or anyone else guessing at my state of mind, the profound doubt that had been with me ever since we had left England. And then it was night. A generator came on. The power it provided went up and down. The bulbs all over the house and the outbuildings constantly dimmed and brightened, and the light they gave seemed to answer a pulse beat, now filling a room, now shrinking back to the walls. I waited all the time that first night for the light to steady itself. At about ten the lights dipped very low. Some minutes later they dipped again, and a while after that they went out. The generator whined down and I was aware of the noise it had been making. There was a ringing in my ears, then something like the sound of crickets in the night, then silence and the dark, the two coming together. Afterwards the pale yellow lights of oil lamps could be seen in the servants' quarters at the back of the house.

I felt very far away from everything I had known, a stranger in that white concrete house with all the strange old Portuguese colonial furniture, the unfamiliar old bathroom fittings; and when I lay down to sleep I saw again—for longer than I had seen them that day—the fantastic rock cones, the straight asphalt road, and the Africans walking.

I drew comfort from Ana, her strength and her authority. And just as now, as you may have noticed, Sarojini, I lean on you, so in those days, ever since she had agreed to my being with her in Africa, I leaned on Ana. I belived in a special way in her luck. Some of this had to do with the very fact that she was a woman who had given herself to me. I believed that she was in some essential way guided and protected, and as long as I was with her no harm could come to me. It may be because of something in our culture that, in spite of appearances, men are really looking for women to lean on. And, of course, if you are not used to governments or the law or society or even history being on your side, then you have to believe in your luck or your star or you will die. I know that you have inherited our mother's uncle's radical genes and have different ideas. I am not going to argue with you. I just want to tell you why I was able to follow someone I hardly knew to a colonial country in Africa of which I knew little except that it had difficult racial and social ideas. I loved Ana and I believed in her luck. The two ideas went together. And since I know, Sarojini, that you have your own ideas about love as well, I will explain. Ana was important to me because I depended on her for my idea of being a man. You know what I mean and I think we can call it love. So I loved Ana, for the great gift she had brought me, and to an equal degree I believed in her luck. I would have gone anywhere with her.

In the sitting room one morning, in that first or second week, I found a little African maid. She was very thin, shiny-faced, and in a flimsy cotton dress. She said, in an overfamiliar but rather stylish way, "So you are Ana's London man." She put her broom against the high upholstered armchair, sat on the chair as on a throne, both her forearms resting flat on the worn upholstered arms of the chair, and began to engage me in polite conversation. She said, as if speaking from a textbook, "Did you have a pleasant journey?" And: "Have you had a chance to see something of the country? What do you think of the country?" I had been studying the language for some time and knew enough of it now to talk in the same stilted way to the little maid. Ana came in. She said, "I wondered who it was." The little maid dropped her grand manner, got up from the chair and took up her broom again. Ana said, "Her father is Júlio. He is the carpenter. He drinks too much."

I had met Júlio. He was a man of mixed race with smiling unreliable eyes, and he lived in the servants' quarters. His drinking was a joke there, and I was to learn not to be too frightened by it. He was a weekend drinker, and often late in the afternoon on a Friday or Saturday or Sunday his African wife would run out to the garden of the main house, quite alone in her terror, moving backwards or sideways step by step, her African cloth slipping off her shoulder, watching all the time for the drunken man in the quarters. This could go on until the light faded. Then the generator would come on, drowning everything with its vibration. The unsteady electric light would further alter the aspect of things; the crisis would pass; and in the quarters in the morning there would be peace again, the passions of the evening washed away.

But it couldn't have been much of a joke for Júlio's daughter. She spoke in her simple and open way of her home life, in those two rooms at the back. She said to me, "When my father gets drunk he beats my mother. Sometimes he beats me too. Sometimes it's so bad I can't sleep. Then I walk up and down the room until I get tired. Sometimes I walk all night." And every night after that, whenever I got into bed, I thought for a second or two about the little maid in the quarters. Another time she said to me, "We eat the same food every day." I didn't know whether she was complaining or boasting or simply speaking a fact about her African ways. In those early days, until local people made me think differently about African girls, I used to worry about Júlio's daughter, seeing myself in her, and wondering how, with all her feelings for fineness as I saw them, she was going to manage in the wilderness in which she found herself.

Of course it wasn't wilderness. It looked open and wild, but it had all been charted and parceled out, and every thirty minutes or so on those dirt roads, if you were driving in a suitable vehicle, you came to an estate house, which was more or less like Ana's. Something in newish white concrete with a wide, bougainvillaea-hung verandah all around, and with additions at the back.

We went one Sunday, not long after we had arrived, to a lunch at one of those neighbours of Ana's. It was a big affair. There were mud-splashed Jeeps and Land Rovers and other four-wheel drives on the sandy open space in front of the house. The African servants wore white uniforms, buttoned at the neck. After drinks people separated according to their inclination, some sitting at the big table in the dining room, others sitting at smaller tables on the verandah, where the tangled old bougainvillaea vines softened the light. I had had no idea what these people would be like and what they would think of me. Ana hadn't talked of the matter and, following her example, I hadn't talked of it to her. I found now that there was no special reaction to me. It was curiously deflating. I was expecting some recognition of my extraordinariness and there was nothing. Some of these estate-owners appeared, in fact, to have no conversation; it was as though the solitude of their lives had taken away that faculty. When eating time came they just sat and ate, husband and wife side by side, not young, not old, people in between in age, eating and not talking, not looking round, very private, as though they were in their own houses. Towards the end of the lunch two or three of these eating women beckoned the servants and talked to them, and after a while the servants came with take-away portions of the lunch in paper bags. It appeared to be a tradition of the place. It might have been that they had come from far, and wanted to have food to eat when they got back home.

Racially they were varied, from what looked like pure white to a deep brown. A number of them were of my father's complexion, and this might have been one reason why they seemed to accept me. Ana said later, "They don't know what to make of you." There were Indians in the country; I wasn't an absolute exotic. There were quite a few Indian traders. They ran cheap shops and socially never stepped outside their families. There was an old and large Goan community, people originally of India, from the very old Portuguese colony there, who had come to this place in Africa to work as clerks and accountants in the civil servants. They spoke Portuguese with a special accent. I couldn't be mistaken for a Goan. My Portuguese was poor and for some reason I spoke it with an English accent. So people couldn't place me and they let me be. I was Ana's London man, as the little housemaid had said.

About the people at the lunch Ana told me afterwards, "They are second-rank Portuguese. That is how they are considered officially, and that is how they consider themselves. They are second rank because most of them have an African grandparent, like me." In those days to be even a second-rank Portuguese was to have a kind of high status, and just as at the lunch they kept their heads down and ate, so in the colonial state they kept their heads down and made what money they could. That was to change in a couple of years, but at the moment that regulated colonial world seemed rock solid to everybody. And that was the world in which, for the first time, I found a complete acceptance.

Those were the days of my intensest love-making with Ana. I loved her—in that room that had been her grandfather's and her mother's, with a view of the nervous branching and fine leaves of the rain tree—for the luck and liberation she had brought me, the undoing of fear, the granting to me of full manhood. I loved, as always, the seriousness of her face at those moments. There was a little curl to her hair just as it sprang out of her temples. In that curl I saw her African ancestry, and loved her for that too. And one day I realized that for all of the past week I had not thought about my fear of losing language and expression, the fear almost of losing the gift of speech.

The estate grew cotton and cashews and sisal. I knew nothing about these crops. But there was a manager and there were overseers. They lived about ten minutes away from the main house, down their own little dirt road, in a cluster of similar little white concrete bungalows with corrugated-iron roofs and small verandahs. Ana had said that the estate needed a man, and I knew, without being told, that my only function was to reinforce Ana's authority with these men. I never tried to do more than that, and the overseers accepted me. I knew that in accepting me they were really respecting Ana's authority. So we all got on. I began to learn. I took pleasure in a way of life that was far from anything I had known or envisaged for myself.

I used to worry in the beginning about the overseers. They didn't seem to have much of a life. They were mixed-race people, born in the country most of them, and they lived in that row of small concrete houses. Only the concrete of their houses separated the overseers from the Africans all around. African thatch and wattle was ordinary; concrete stood for dignity. But concrete wasn't a true barrier. These overseers lived, really, with the Africans. No other way was open to them. I used to think, trying to put myself in their place, that with their mixed background they might have felt the need of something more. There was the town on the coast. It offered a different kind of life, but it was more than an hour away in daylight and a good deal more after dark. It was a place only for quick excursions. To work on the estate was to live on the estate, and it was known that many of the overseers had African families. Whatever face these men showed us, the life waiting for them at home, in their concrete houses, was an African life at which I could only guess.

One day, when I was driving with one of the overseers to a new cotton field, I began to talk to the man about his life. We were in a Land Rover, and we had left the dirt road and were driving through the bush, avoiding the bigger boggy dips and the dead branches of felled trees. I was expecting to hear some story of unfulfilled ambition from the overseer, some story of things going wrong, expecting to catch some little resentment of people better off and in the world outside. But there was no resentment. The overseer thought himself blessed. He had tried living in Portugal; he had even tried living in a South African town; he had come back. He hit the steering wheel of the Land Rover with the heel of his palm and said, "I can't live anywhere else." When I asked why, he said, "This. What we are doing now. You can't do this in Portugal." Land Rovers and four-wheel drives were new to me; I was still excited myself to drive off a road and pick a way through hummocky wet bush. But I felt that the overseer had a larger appreciation of the life of the place; his surrender was more than the simple sexual thing it seemed. And when I next saw the mildewed white staff bungalows I looked at them with a new respect. So bit by bit I learned. Not only about cotton and sisal and cashew, but also about people.

I got used to the road to the town. I knew the giant rock cones along the way. Each cone had its own shape and was a marker for me. Some cones rose clean out of the ground; some had a rock debris at their base where a face of the cone had flaked off; some cones were grey and bare; some had yellowish lichen on one side; on the ledges of some which had flaked there was vegetation, sometimes even a tree. The cones were always new. It was always an adventure, after a week or two on the estate, to drive to the town. For an hour or so it always seemed new: the colonial shops, the rustic, jumbled shop windows, the African loaders sitting outside the shops waiting for a loading job; the paved streets, the cars and trucks, the garages; the mixed population, with the red-faced young Portuguese conscripts of our little garrison giving a strange air of Europe to the place. The garrison was as yet very small; and the barracks were still small and plain and unthreatening, low two-storey buildings in white or grey concrete, of a piece with the rest of the town. Sometimes there was a new café to go to. But cafés didn't last in our town. The conscripts didn't have money, and the townspeople preferred to live privately.

Most of the shops we used were Portuguese. One or two were Indian. I was nervous of going into them at first. I didn't want to get that look from the shop people that would remind me of home and bad things. But there was never anything like that, no flicker of racial recognition from the family inside. There, too, they accepted the new person I had become in Ana's country. They seemed not to know that I was once something else. There, too, they kept their heads down and did what they had to do. So that for me, as for the overseers, though in different ways, the place offered an extra little liberation.

* * *

Questions for Discussion and Writing

1. Why was Willie able to leave everything and go to a colonial country in Africa?
2. V.S. Naipul is known for his succinct and graceful writing style. Read a favorite passage that elucidates the search for identity.
3. What part of himself, his identity, does he seek from his relationship with Ana?
4. Describe the lunch that they are invited to at one of Ana's neighbors.
5. What do you think it meant to Willie to be "Ana's London man" in Africa?
6. How was Willie important to Ana?
7. In this excerpt, the author focuses on Willie forming his identity, especially his sense of masculinity, through his relationship with Ana. Show where this is evident in the text.
8. In your teaching, when have you known the family relationship to be important to the student's identity? Give an example.

Dreams of Trespass by Fatima Mernissi

Fatima Mernissi was born in a harem in Fez, Morocco. In her memoir, she describes what life was like behind the iron gates of a domestic harem. This world, very foreign to Western women, is an extended family whose members are female. Though restricted, it is a world of security and the familiar. It is like a prison in that there are no windows. Women are not allowed to leave without a chaperone. Although the women accept their lot, they applaud gains in freedom for women in other Muslim countries. There in the company of women, Fatima creates a strong inner world in which she had an important freedom, the freedom to imagine different realities. However, once a year, Fatima was allowed to leave the harem. In the excerpted passage, she describes the experience and how it affected her sense of identity and her inner goals and dreams.

From *Dreams of Trespass* by Fatima Mernissi

Our harem in Fez was surrounded by high walls and, with the exception of the little square chunk of sky that you could see from the courtyard below, nature did not exist. Of course, if you rushed like an arrow up to the terrace, you could see that the sky was larger than the house, larger than everything, but from the courtyard, nature seemed irrelevant. It had been replaced by geometric and floral designs reproduced on tiles, woodwork, and stucco. The only strikingly beautiful flowers we had in the house were those of the colorful brocades which covered the sofas and those of the embroidered silk drapes that sheltered the doors and windows. You could not, for example, open a shutter to look outside when you wanted to escape. All the windows opened onto the courtyard. There were none facing the street.

Once a year, during springtime, we went on a *nzaha,* or picnic, at my uncle's farm in Oued Fez, ten kilometers from the city. The important adults rode in cars, while the children, divorced aunts, and other relatives were put into two big trucks rented for the occasion. Aunt Habiba and Chama always carried tambourines, and they would make such a hell of a noise along the way that the truck driver would go crazy. "If you ladies don't stop this," he would shout, "I'm going to drive off the road and throw everyone into the valley." But his threats always came to nothing, because his voice would be drowned out by the tambourines and hand clapping.

On picnic day, everyone woke up at dawn and buzzed around the courtyard as if it were a religious festival day with groups of people organizing food here, drinks there, and putting drapes and carpets into bundles everywhere. Chama and Mother took care of the swings. "How can you have a picnic without swings?" they would argue whenever Father suggested they forget about them for once, because it took so much time to hang them from the trees. "Besides," he would add, just to provoke Mother, "swings are fine for children, but when heavy grownups are involved, the poor trees might suffer." While father talked and waited for Mother to get angry, she would just keep on packing up the swings and the ropes to tie them with, without a single glance in his direction. Chama would sing aloud, "If men can't tie the swings / women will do it / Lallallalla," imitating the high-pitched melody of our national anthem "Maghribuna watanuna" (Our Morocco, Our Homeland).* Meanwhile, Samir and I would be feverishly looking for our espadrilles, for there was no help to be had from our mothers, so involved were they in their own projects, and Lalla Mani would be counting the number of glasses and plates "just to evaluate the damage, and see how many will be broken by the end of the day." She could do without the picnic, she often said, especially since as far as tradition was concerned, its origin was dubious. "There's no record of it in the Hadith," she said, "It might even be counted as a sin on Judgment Day."**

We would arrive on the farm in mid-morning, equipped with dozens of carpets and light sofas and *khanouns.*** Once the carpets had been unfolded, the light sofas would be spread out, the charcoal fires lit, and the shish kebabs grilled. The teakettles would sing along with the birds. Then, after lunch, some of the women would scatter into the woods and fields, searching for flowers, herbs, and other kinds of plants to use in their beauty treatments. Others would take turns on the swings. Only after sunset would we make the journey back

---

*Maghrib is the Arabic name for Morocco, the land of the setting sun, from *gharb* (west).

**The Hadith is a compilation of the Prophet Mohammed's deeds and sayings. Recorded and written down after his death, the Hadith is considered to be one of the primary sources of Islam, the first being the Koran, the book revealed directly by Allah to his Prophet.

***Khanouns are portable charcoal fire containers, the Moroccan equivalent of the barbecue grill. They can be made of pottery or metal.

to the house, and the gate would be closed behind us. And for days after that, Mother would feel miserable. "When you spend a whole day among trees," she would say, "waking up with walls as horizons becomes unbearable."

You could not get into our house, except by passing through the main gate controlled by Ahmed the doorkeeper. But you could get out a second way, by using the roof-level terrace. You could jump from our terrace to the neighbors' next door, and then go out to the street through their door. Officially, our terrace key was kept in Lalla Mani's possession, with Ahmed turning off the lights to the stairs after sunset. But because the terrace was constantly being used for all kinds of domestic activities throughout the day, from retrieving olives that were stored in big jars up there, to washing and drying clothes, the key was often left with Aunt Habiba, who lived in the room right next to the terrace.

The terrace exit route was seldom watched, for the simple reason that getting from it to the street was a difficult undertaking. You needed to be quite good at three skills, climbing, jumping, and agile landing. Most of the women could climb up and jump fairly well, but not many could land gracefully. So, from time to time, someone would come in with a bandaged ankle, and everyone would know just what she'd been up to. The first time I came down from the terrace with bleeding knees, Mother explained to me that a woman's chief problem in life was figuring out how to land. "Whenever you are about to embark on an adventure," she said, "you have to think about the landing. Not about the takeoff. So whenever you feel like flying, think about how and where you'll end up."

But there was also another, more solemn reason why women like Chama and Mother did not consider escaping from the terrace to be a viable alternative to using the front gate. The terrace route had a clandestine, covert dimension to it, which was repulsive to those who were fighting for the principle of a woman's right to free movement. Confronting Ahmed at the gate was a heroic act. Escaping from the terrace was not, and did not carry with it that inspiring, subversive flame of liberation.

None of this intrigue applied, of course, to Yasmina's farm. The gate had hardly any meaning, because there were no walls. And to be in a harem, I thought, you needed a barrier, a frontier. That summer, when I visited Yasmina, I told her what Chama had said about how harems got started. When I saw that she was listening, I decided to show off all my historical knowledge, and started talking about the Romans and their harems, and how the Arabs became the sultans of the planet thanks to Caliph Harun al-Rashid's one thousand women, and how the Christians tricked the Arabs by changing the rules on them while they were asleep. Yasmina laughed a lot when she heard the story, and said that she was too illiterate to evaluate the historical facts, but that it all sounded very funny and logical too. I then asked her if what Chama had said was true or false, and Yasmina said that I needed to relax about this right-and-wrong business. She said that there were things which could be both, and things which could be neither. "Words are like onions," she said. "The more skins you peel off, the more meanings you encounter. And when you start discovering multiplicities of meanings, then right and wrong becomes irrelevant. All these questions about harems that you and Samir have been asking are all fine and good, but there will always be more to be discovered." And then she added, "I am going to peel one more skin for you now. But remember, it is only one among others."

The word, "harem," she said, was a slight variation of the word *haram*, the forbidden, the proscribed. It was the opposite of *halal*, the permissible. Harem was the place where a man sheltered his family, his wife or wives, and children and relatives. It could be a house or a tent, and it referred both to the space and to the people who lived within it. One said "Sidi So-and-So's harem," referring both to his family members and to his physical home. One thing that helped me see this more clearly was when Yasmina explained that Mecca was a space where behavior was strictly codified. The moment you stepped inside, you were bound by laws and regulations. People who entered Mecca had to be pure; they had to perform purification rituals and refrain from lying, cheating, and doing harmful deeds. The city belonged to Allah and you had to obey his *shari'a*, or sacred law, if you entered his territory. The same thing applied to a harem when it was a house belonging to a man. No other men could enter it without the owner's permission, and when they did, they had to obey his rules. A harem was about private space and the rules regulating it. In addition, Yasmina said, it did not need walls. Once you knew what was forbidden, you carried the harem within. You had it in your head, "inscribed under your forehead and under your skin." That idea of an invisible harem, a law tattooed in the mind, was frightfully unsettling to me. I did not like it at all, and I wanted her to explain more.

The farm, said Yasmina, was a harem, although it did not have walls. "You only need walls, if you have streets!" But, if you decided, like Grandfather, to live in the countryside, then you didn't need gates, because you were in the middle of the fields and there were no passersby. Women could go freely out into the fields, because there were no strange men hovering around, peeping at them. Women could walk or ride for hours without seeing a soul. But if by chance they did meet a male peasant along the way, and he saw that they were unveiled, he would cover his head with the hood of his own *djellaba* to show that he was not looking. So in this case, Yasmina said, the harem was in the peasant's head, inscribed somewhere under his forehead. He knew that the women on the farm belonged to Grandfather Tazi, and that he had no right to look at them.

This business of going around with a frontier inside the head disturbed me, and discreetly I put my hand to my forehead to make sure it was smooth, just to see if by any chance I might be harem-free. But then, Yasmina's explanation got even more alarming, because the next thing she said was that any space you entered had its own invisible rules, and you needed to figure them out. "And when I say space," she continued, "it can be any space—a courtyard, a terrace, or a room, or even the street for that matter. Wherever there are human beings, there is a *qa'ida,* or invisible rule. If you stick to the *qa'ida,* nothing bad can happen to you." In Arabic, she reminded me, *qa'ida* meant many different things, all of which shared the same basic premise. A mathematical law or legal system was *qa'ida,* and so was the foundation of a building. *Qa'ida* was also a custom, or a behavioral code. *Qa'ida* was everywhere. Then she added something which really scared me: "Unfortunately, most of the time, the *qa'ida* is against women."

"Why?" I asked. "That's not fair, is it?" And I crept closer so as not to miss a word of her answer. The world, Yasmina said, was not concerned about being fair to women. Rules were made in such a manner as to deprive them in some way or another. For example, she said, both men and women worked from dawn until very late at night. But men made money and women did not. That was one of the invisible rules. And when a woman worked hard, and was not making money, she was stuck in a harem, even though she could not see its walls. "Maybe the rules are ruthless because they are not made by women," was Yasmina's final comment. "But why aren't they made by women?" I asked. "The moment women get smart and start asking that very question," she replied, "instead of dutifully cooking and washing dishes all the time, they will find a way to change the rules and turn the whole planet upside down." "How long will it take?" I asked, and Yasmina said, "A long time."

* * *

Questions for Discussion and Writing

1. How did her summer make the author redefine the definition of the harem?
2. What is the background of the concept of harem? (Access the Internet, or go to the library and research this concept of family organization.)
3. Why was it not significant that there were no walls on the farm?
4. What lesson did her Aunt Yasmina try to teach Mernissi, and why was it significant since we know the author went on to become a writer and sociologist teaching at University Mohammed V, and a leader in women's rights?
5. Describe the trip to her uncle's farm in Oued Fez. How do you think the trip had an effect on the author's developing identity?
6. *Osama* (2003) is an award-winning film about a young girl who pretends to be a boy in Aghanistan. Rent the film, and discuss what connections it has with this excerpt.
7. What do we learn about women, identity, and culture from this excerpt?

My Invented Country by Isabel Allende

Just as Mernissi gained a different perspective in leaving the harem, when an individual leaves the familiar and journeys to a new and different place, his or her perspective changes. In the following excerpt, Isabel Allende, now a world-famous author, describes returning to Chile for a visit and returning to San Francisco and how a this border crossing has affected her life. She has developed a new voice as an exiled Chilean because of a political coup in which her life was in danger. She described it as a closed society in which there is very little room for developing a unique voice. In contrast, in San Francisco, she was able to develop her voice, a hybrid, cosmopolitan one in which she gains the agency over her life that she would have never had in Chile living under her grandfather's roof. Read her description of this in the excerpted passage.

From *My Invented Country* by Isabel Allende

In 1994 I went back to Chile, looking for inspiration, a trip I have since repeated yearly. I found my compatriots more relaxed and the democracy stronger, although conditioned by the presence of a still-powerful military and by the senators Pinochet had appointed for life in order to control the Congress. The government had to maintain a delicate balance among the political and social forces. I went to working-class neighborhoods where people had once been contentious and organized. The progressive priests and nuns who had lived among the poor all those years told me that the poverty was the same but that the solidarity had disappeared, and that now crime and drugs, which had become the most serious problem among the young—had been added to the issues of alcoholism, domestic violence, and unemployment.

The rules to live by were: try to forget the past, work for the future, and don't provoke the military for any reason. Compared to the rest of Latin America, Chile was living in a good moment of political and economic stability; even so, five million people were still below the poverty level. Except for the victims of repression, their families, and a few organizations that kept a watch out for civil rights violations, no one spoke the words *disappeared* or *torture* aloud. That situation changed when Pinochet was arrested in London, where he had gone for a medical check-up and to collect his commission for an arms deal. A Spanish judge charged him with murdering Spanish citizens, and requested his extradition from England to Spain. The general, who still counted on the unconditional support of the armed forces, had for twenty-five years been isolated by the adulators who always congregate around power. He had been warned of the risks of travel abroad, but he went anyway, confident of his impunity. His surprise at being arrested by the British can be compared only to that of everyone in Chile, long accustomed to the idea that he was untouchable. By chance, I was in Santiago when that occurred, and I witnessed how within the course of a week a Pandora's box was opened and all the things that had been hidden beneath layers and layers of silence began to emerge. In those first days there were turbulent street demonstrations by Pinochet's supporters, who threatened nothing less than a declaration of war against England or a commando raid to rescue the prisoner. The nation's press, frightened, wrote of the insult to the Esteemed Senator-for-Life and to the honor and sovereignty of the nation, but a week later demonstrations in his support had become minimal, the military were keeping mute, and the tone had changed in the media: now they referred to the "ex-dictator, arrested in London." No one believed that the English would hand over the prisoner to be tried in Spain, which in fact didn't happen, but in Chile the fear that was still in the air diminished rapidly. The military lost prestige and power in a matter of days. The tacit agreement to bury the truth was over, thanks to the actions of that Spanish judge.

On that trip I traveled through the south. Again I lost myself in the prodigious nature of my country and met with faithful friends to whom I am closer than to my brothers; in Chile, friendship is forever. I returned to California renewed and ready to work. I assigned myself a subject as far removed from death as possible and wrote *Aphrodite,* some ramblings about gluttony and lust, the only cardinal sins worth paying a penance for. I bought a ton of cookbooks and quite a few about eroticism, and I made excursions to the gay district of San Francisco, where for several weeks I scavenged through the pornography shops. (That kind of investigation would have been difficult in Chile. On the off chance that such material existed, I would never have dared buy it: it would have placed my family's honor in jeopardy.) I learned a lot. It's a shame that I acquired this knowledge so late in my life, when I don't have anyone to practice with: Willie made it clear that he is not disposed to hanging a trapeze from the ceiling.

That book helped me emerge from the depression I had sunk into with the death of my daughter. Since that time I have written a book a year. I'm never short on ideas, only time. With Chile and California in mind, I wrote *Daughter of Fortune* and *Portrait in Sepia,* books in which the characters travel back and forth between my two countries.

In conclusion, I want to add that the United States has treated me very well. It has allowed me to be myself, or any version of self it has occurred to me to create. The entire world passes through San Francisco, each person carrying his or her cargo of memories and hopes. This city is filled with foreigners; I am not an exception. In the streets you hear a thousand tongues, temples are raised for all denominations, and the scent of food from the most remote points of the world fills the air. Few people are born here, most are strangers in paradise, as I am. It doesn't matter to anyone who I am or what I do; no one watches me or judges me, they leave me in peace. The negative side of that is that if I drop dead in the street, no one will notice but, in the end, that is a cheap price to pay for liberty. In California the only thing that isn't tolerated is intolerance.

My grandson Alejandro's observation about the three years I have left to live forces me to ask myself whether I want to live them in the United States or return to Chile. I don't know the answer. Frankly, I doubt that I would leave my house in California. I visit Chile once or twice a year, and when I arrive a lot of people seem happy to see me, though I think they're even happier when I leave—including my mother, who lives in fear that her daughter will do something foolish, for example, appear on television talking about abortion. I feel great for a few days, but after two or three weeks I begin to miss tofu and green tea.

This book has helped me understand that I am not obligated to make a decision: I can have one foot in Chile and another here, that's why we have planes, and I am not among those who are afraid to fly because of terrorism. I have a fatalistic attitude: no one dies one minute before or one minute after the prescribed time. For the moment California is my home and Chile is the land of my nostalgia. My heart isn't divided, it has merely grown larger. I can live and write anywhere. Every book contributes to the completion of that "country inside my head," as my grandchildren call it. In the slow practice of writing, I have fought with my demons and obsessions, I have explored the corners of memory, I have dredged up stories and people from oblivion, I have stolen others' lives, and from all this raw material I have constructed a land that I call my country. That is where I come from.

I hope that this long commentary answers the stranger's question about nostalgia. Don't believe everything I say: I tend to exaggerate and, as I warned at the beginning, I can't be objective where Chile is concerned. Let's just say, to be completely honest, that I can't be objective, period. In any case, what's most important doesn't appear in my biography or my books, it happens in a nearly imperceptible way in the secret chambers of the heart. I am a writer because I was born with a good ear for stories, and I was lucky enough to have an eccentric family and the destiny of a wanderer. The profession of literature has defined me. Word by word I have created the person I am and the invented country in which I live.

* * *

Questions for Discussion and Writing

1. What are the benefits for Allende, as a writer and as a person, of going to San Francisco?
2. What was it like going to her native country in 1994?
3. Why do you think that it benefits a writer to leave the place written about, in terms of perspective?
4. What does she mean by "California is my home and Chile is the land of my nostalgia"? Do you think Allende feels she has a divided self, or that she has successfully acculturated to the culture in California?
5. Later on in her book, Allende says that her memory transforms reality and changes the way things really are. She says in many ways she has recreated Chile, making it a mythic place. How do you think this might happen?
6. How can writing help with the acculturation process?

Polite Lies by Kyoko Mori

Having moved to the United States has profoundly affected Kyoko Mori's perspective and sense of self. In the excerpted passage from *Polite Lies*, her memoir, Mori discusses the lack of personal choice in Japan. The author, who has acculturated to the United States, sees the difference between two lifestyles, particularly where color and gender are concerned. In Japan, there is no personal choice when it comes to what colors women should wear. The rules are rigid, and women are accepted only when they follow the dress code. In this passage, Mori discusses how her perceptions have changed since she has immigrated to America and how hard it is for her to express her identity when she returns to Japan to visit. She resents the restriction and presents an impression of an outsider, but she is excused for having this attitude since the Japanese there make allowances for a woman who has lived in the United States.

From *Polite Lies* by Kyoko Mori

Although I did not fully understand the importance of everyday symbolism until I was an adult, I always noticed the way people in Japan fell into uncomfortable silence when they saw someone dressed in the wrong color. Even as children, we were taught that boys must never wear pink or red, and that we should not sit next to a man in a purple or yellow shirt on the train because he is probably a *yakuza* or a foreigner. There were rules about what colors everyone should wear according to their age and gender, and people who did not obey these rules were sure to be up to no good.

When I came to America, I was relieved that the rules about colors were much more relaxed. Americans tend to dress their boy babies in powder blue and their girl babies in pale pink, but some people shun this practice as sexist. American business executives prefer navy blue and avoid colors that are regarded as frivolous, not fit for business attire: certain shades of pink, lavender, or red, colors traditionally associated with femininity. But the hockey coach at our college wears a pale pink cardigan now and then, and my friend Fred buys women's singlets and shorts for running because he looks bad in dark colors marketed for men. No one labels the hockey coach or Fred as suspicious characters or considers them to be eccentric. In Japan, to appear in the "wrong" color just once is to be branded as someone who doesn't know or care what is right and proper.

The color rules are fairly easy for Japanese men. All they have to do is avoid reds and pinks as young boys and then settle into a wardrobe of navy, black, and white when they grow up to be businessmen. Women have more choices, but in Japan, having choices usually means having more ways to go wrong.

As soon as I was old enough to learn the names of colors in kindergarten, I became aware that there were old-woman colors and young-woman colors, as well as boy colors and girl colors. The differences between old-woman colors and young-woman colors seemed much more complicated than those between boy colors and girl colors. From the way my mother complained about her mother's clothes, I could see that they didn't agree about how strictly my grandmother should follow the rules.

"Your grandmother dresses too much like an old woman," my mother often said when we went shopping. "I would love to buy that dark green wool and knit her a sweater, but she'll never wear it. She only likes clothes that are very *jimi*."

Jimi means, literally, "earth-taste," though it does not refer to what Westerners think of as earth tones. The word is used to refer to colors that are subdued: dark gray, dark brown, navy blue. As far back as I can remember, Fuku wore these colors exclusively, in house dresses and blouse-skirt combinations that were large and shapeless. The only "good" clothes she had were the formal black kimonos with the family crest embroidered in white. She wore the kimonos only to weddings or funerals. My mother, who wanted her mother to look a little "more modern," would send her dresses she had sewn herself. The dresses were by no means bright or flashy: modest cotton or wool A-lines in silver-gray, cobalt blue, or maybe maroon if my mother was feeling hopeful that Fuku would change.

Maroon was as daring as an old woman could dress. My mother was careful not to send anything inappropriate; still, the new clothes stayed in Fuku's dresser drawers. They were too beautiful to wear, Fuku insisted. Every time we visited, my mother was depressed to see the clothes neatly folded and stored, never worn.

The old-woman colors looked and sounded depressing to me. In Japanese, even their names are dismal. *Nezumi-iro* (mouse color) for dark gray; *cha-iro* (tea color) for dark brown; *hai-iro* (ash color) for white gray. The names reminded me of bleak farm kitchens. Sooner or later, everyone obeyed the rules and resigned themselves to these dismal sounding colors. Even my mother complied when it came to her turn. In her mid-thirties, she gave away several of her dresses and suits to her younger sister and sisters-in-law, saying they were too *hade* ("stick-out" and "flashy")—the opposite of jimi—for her. The clothes she gave away weren't in colors I now think of as bright. By the time my mother was my mother, she no longer wore bright pinks, reds, or yellows, the colors of childhood and youth. When she became thirty-five, even light blue (which has a beautiful name in Japanese: *mizu-iro,* "water color") and forest green (*midori,* another pretty-sounding name, sometimes used as a woman's name) were too *hade.* She was supposed to move on to the browns and dark blues, and in ten years, she would have to give up even these colors and wear only the grays and the darkest blues.

My mother was forty-one when she killed herself. She never completed her transition into the brown-and-dark-blue middle age. She was a woman who spent her weekends viewing the Impressionists, who stayed up past midnight embroidering pink flowers and delicate yellow butterflies on my blouses. In her dresser drawers, she left boxes of embroidery floss, in colors she could no longer wear. A month after her death, I began seventh grade at a private girls' school—the only junior high school in the Kobe-Osaka area that didn't require uniforms. For the first-day ceremony at the school, I wore a red dress my mother had made for me.

∗ ∗ ∗

Questions for Discussion and Writing

1. Why is the author allowed to be different when she goes to Japan to visit?
2. What role does personal appearance play in Japan? How does this differ from the American culture?
3. How does the role of color in Japan reflect the Japanese attitude toward gender differences? Can you think of other cultures where color is used in similar ways?
4. In her book, Mori says that the individual freedom is sacrificed for the good of the individual group. Do you think this is beneficial for society?
5. Can you compare other values that symbolize status in society?
6. Each culture has its own value system. Rent the movie *The Terminal.* In it, Tom Hanks plays an immigrant who came to the United States just to get a signature of a famous jazz musician for his father, and he finds all kinds of obstacles are put in his way. After you see the movie, make a chart of contrasting differences between the protagonist and representatives of other cultures.

More about Identity and Literature

In the previous excerpts, we have seen how very complex culture and identity can be. In reading the texts by Smith, McBride, and Lahiri, we saw how hair, skin, and a person's name can vividly influence self-perception.

Very often we learn to grow toward that person whom we eventually will become through close family relationships and through context. In Mernissi's autobiography, she is inspired through the strong role models she encountered in her mother and Aunt Chama, whereas Naipul explored his identity as a man through his loving relationship with his wife, Ana.

We also change and grow as a result of a change in our location. Just as Mernissi was deeply influenced by leaving the walls of the harem in the family picnic, so was Isabel Allende by leaving her native Chile and becoming a resident of San Francisco. By becoming an exiled author, she gained a fresh perspective on her native country. Similarly, writer Mori has been able to see cultural differences with regard to color symbolism in Japan after having lived in the United States for many years.

Other underlying themes present in these texts are the social backgrounds of class and socioeconomics. There is also the sense of agency of choice as demonstrated by Gogol when he decided to change his name to Nikhil.

As we live our lives, we learn. In the learning, changes occur. Identity is revised accordingly. We are, in many respects, all immigrants. One could argue that we are all exiled at birth, and we all embrace new experiences everyday. As the context changes, an individual must make new choices every day. Karen Armstrong, in her autobiography *The Spiral Staircase*, described the culture shock and disorientation that she experienced when she left the convent and became a student in the '60s. She felt lost the way an immigrant from another country might feel. For immigrants, the choices are obviously more extreme since they are not able to read the contexts against which decisions have to be made and identities forged. And often, especially where children and political exiles are concerned, they were not able to choose where they wanted to live.

Second language learners have trouble finding a way to represent who they feel they are. The identity that each individual has is not a static thing, but multi-faceted and ongoing. A learner may be a mother, social activist, and a teacher, and each of these roles affects the voice discovered in a second language. Each may signal a different way of behaving (Ivanic

& Camps, 2001), including expression of speaking and writing. Too often, second language learners find they are stereotyped and the complexity of their human identities ignored, especially at school.

Literature and reading can help second language learners find a sense of identity and voice. Reading a text can help form a kind of neutral territory in which new identities are tried out and old ones discarded. In *Reading Lolita in Tehran,* Nafisi described the transformation that took place when her students came to her apartment in Teheran to read western classics, like Nabokov's *Lolita.* There, they would take off their head scarves, let their hair hang loose, and enjoy freedom they would not find in the outside world. They would also find and make connections to Lolita or wander into the world of Fitzgerald's Gatsby, which changed their consciousness forever. They also read James's *Daisy Miller.* Nafisi writes of their reaction: "Daisy was the character my female students most identified with. Some of them became obsessed. Later in my workshop, they go back to her time and again, speaking of her courage, something they felt they had lacked. Mahsid and Mitra spoke of her with regret in their writing; like Winterbourne, they felt they were bound to make a mistake about her. . . . All the fuss we made over these writers, as if what they said was a matter of life and death to us—James and Bronte and Nabokov and Jane Austen" (Nafisi, p. 333). Clearly, the reading of fiction allowed the group freedom that they did not have in their lives.

Whether from a repressive regime or a real prison, the transforming power of literature can be felt. In Jean Trounstine's book *Shakespeare Behind Bars,* women at the Framingham Prison created a world where the participants felt free to express themselves through the medium of reading Shakespeare. By stepping into the shoes of Shakespeare's character, whether Macbeth or King Lear, the women tried on new perspectives that made their incarceration tolerable. In addition, the cathartic effect of the great tragedies and the lightheartedness of the comedies helped them psychologically. The expressiveness helped them feel that their sense of agency was not forever gone, not at least in the created world of art (Troustine, p. 255).

Susan Florio-Ruane in *Teacher Education and the Cultural Imagination* writes about the transforming power of literature on her book groups, whether they were novice teachers or veterans. She describes the discussions the reading engenders and how it brings awareness of context and culture into the teaching professions. This knowledge can be extended to how great story-telling can affect one's ability to craft one's own story and inner development. There is obviously then more to book club–type of activities than what might be apparent.

In Nydia Flores-Gonzalez' *School Kids/Street Kids*, the author discusses whether forming an identity connected with learning and school or an identity with the outside world is critical as to whether or not students continue as students. In her chapter on ways to keep students' identity aligned with the school, she mentions the importance of connecting and incorporating their school identity with other identities that interest them (Flores-Gonzales, p. 155). This could be accomplished by a student reading (book) club. The reading of literature in which students can find aspects of themselves, whether in Toni Morrison's *The Bluest Eye* or Edith Wharton's *Ethan Frome,* is one way that students can create a neutral ground of shared experience that makes school meaningful. They can become enriched and nurtured in a risk-free school environment without leaving their other identities behind. They can experience narrative as a way of knowing and learn to explore context as an important variable in discovering any kind of truth. They learn that everything worth knowing has a story and exists in context.

In the next chapters, we will examine ethnographic interviews in a graduate class of an urban university, which will give us another kind of evidence as to the complexity of change and identity.

Questions for Discussion and Writing

1. Turn to a partner and tell him or her which excerpt you preferred because you connected with it in some way. Be specific in your explanation.
2. Now tell the class what excerpt surprised you the most. What did you learn or see in a new way?
3. Write a journal entry about a book or poem that influenced you in a significant way. Tell how and why it affected you.
4. Optional Activity: Choose one of the excerpted books and read the whole book. Then write a summary and response paper.

CHAPTER 6

Ethnography: The Interview

L ife histories, fiction, and poetry based on real-life experience
provide excellent ways to understand a person and his or her
reality, including the cultural context. Chapters 1–5 have dealt
with this mode of understanding the self through reading literature; the
process of acculturation as adaptation; the sense of agency and mastery of
the environment; as well as confusion, anomie, and loss. However, there
are many ways to unearth a story. In the qualitative research paradigm,
ethnography, including the ethnographic interview, provides a valid means
of understanding an individual perspective.

The goal of ethnography is to provide a description of a cultural
phenomenon. For example, in education, in order to research a teaching
method, the researcher may take a role of participant observer of a
classroom. Then, guided by the research question or hypothesis, data will
be gathered and triangulated by audiotaping, videotaping, and keeping a
researcher's log. In addition, data can be gathered by using an ethnographic
interview, which is usually written in the native language of the researcher.
However, interviews are usually conducted in the native language of the
informant whenever possible.

According to Spradley (1979), a broader goal of ethnography is to
gain understanding of the human species (p. 16). If the researcher does

not speak the native language of the informant, it is important that the researcher learn how to understand key terms in the language of the informant. This use of language enables the researcher to understand the world of the interviewee, insofar as language gives form to that individual's thought.

Researchers are encouraged to follow the Principals of Professional Responsibility as outlined by the Council of the American Anthropological Association. Generally, this means they must be mindful of the rights of the person being interviewed and try to maintain privacy. The informant has the right to read the interview or research project when it is done. Care is taken to obtain access and protect the privacy of the people who are the subjects of the study. A statement must be signed granting permission, and the goals of the study and interview must be made clear to the participants. (See Appendix 2 for a version of the form.)

What makes a good informant? In the example from my graduate class, an informant is someone who is willing to share his or her culture and at the same time allow the beginning ethnographer to practice interview skills. Interviews with close family members or someone with whom the interviewee has an intimate relationship are discouraged because the objectivity needed for research will be lacking. Very young children will be more difficult because of the lack of verbal fluency; videotaping might be a better medium. An informant can be anyone outside of these two classes of people, an ordinary person with ordinary knowledge. Anyone can be an informant and provide interviews that communicate knowledge, depending on the researcher's question or the problem that is guiding the research. What the researcher is trying to find out will determine the questions he or she uses; furthermore, the language used should be the authentic vocabulary evoked in that particular context.

When the researcher uses the ethnographic interview, the person interviewed will project all kinds of relationships into the ethnographer-interviewee relationships. The interviewee will think of the interviewer as friend, employer, or any of the other identities he or she might possess. At this point, the interviewer should be truthful as to the purpose of the research and the reason for the interview. The ethnographic interviewer sets aside cultural boundaries, and by using the language of the informant, attempts to uncover the world of the person being interviewed authentically. This in-depth view of a person's reality and life story is in no way similar to a survey questionnaire. The researcher's point of view in this paradigm of research will encourage the kind of open-ended questioning technique that helps the interviewer understand the interviewee's world. These questions include contrast questions that search for ideas that might be meaningful in the interviewee's world by asking for examples and specific words to describe experience (Spradley, pp. 155–160).

The informant is encouraged to answer questions naturally, not in an analytic way. First, the informant is given an explanation for the interview and research, and the purpose for the interview is given. Then, permission should be asked to tape the interview. However, I strongly suggest letting the interview begin without the tape recorder; the interviewer should have it ready nearby. After the question and answers have begun, the tape recorder should be turned on unobtrusively without interrupting the flow of language. For examples of questions in an ethnographic interview, see Chapter 7.

How is the interview different from a conversation? There are several characteristics of the ethnographic interview. The interview questions are designed to elicit information of a cultural nature. Another difference is the stated purpose for the interview, which is shared with the informant. In addition, there tends to be more repetition with the ethnographic interview and more encouragement to expand and develop ideas. The interviewer will express ignorance about not knowing the world of the informer, thus encouraging more verbalization so that more will be learned about the informant's world. For example, many questions may be asked for description of a place or a task (Lofland and Lofland, 1984, pp. 25–30).

If you tape an interview, you do not need to record all of it. You may switch it on and off. Or, you may choose to record the entire interview. Transcribing an entire interview may be time consuming, but the information gleaned will be worth the effort.

Field notes must be taken. In this case, they will be the interviewer's journal. In it the thoughts, analysis, comments, or questions can be written. The best method is to record verbatim exactly what the informant says and transcribe it. Next to the transcription, write the comments of the researcher. This kind of double entry helps the researcher understand which language is the informant's and which language is the analysis of the researcher. Each field notes or journal entry should be dated. Be sure to keep your researcher's log updated, ideally before and after interviews. Write down any ideas that come to you regarding the interviewer or topics taped in the interview. See the interviews and interview journal on pages 96–100 for a model.

Then, having gathered information from the interview, you will go over the transcripts and tapes many times in order to discover *themes,* or *underlying principles,* that run through the interview. These are ideas that keep cropping up in the transcripts of the interviews, field notes, and taped segments. In Chapter 7, you will see themes gleaned from a research project conducted with a Graduate Class of Applied Linguistics.

The ethnographer should examine the data, looking for these themes. Chapter 7 demonstrates themes that were collected from the data, the interviews my graduate students conducted on topics about immigration and identity issues.

Questions for Discussion and Writing

1. What are your research questions? What do you hope to learn from the interviews?
2. Write a list of questions that you would like to ask the informant.
3. Which people do you know who have bicultural identities who would be good informants?
4. What issues do you anticipate for your role as interviewer?
5. How will you ensure anonymity of the interviewee?
6. Free-write your first entry of your interviewer's log.

CHAPTER 7

Stories of Border Crossings and Identity Changes

This chapter contains a discussion of the results of ethnographic interviews conducted as part of a class assignment. After having studied the material in Chapter 6 on how to conduct an ethnographic interview, my graduate students in a course in applied linguistics were asked to select an informant who was a bilingual adult or teenager and interview him or her about their story and how it influenced identity. Stated as a question it was: *How has moving to another country influenced [the individual's] identity? What other factors came into play in determining acculturation and adaptation to this country, both negative and positive aspects? What decisions were made that impacted the individual's lives, especially those that were particularly empowering, allowing the immigrant agency and control?*

The students were to select an appropriate informant and obtain permission for the interview (see Appendix B). Interview questions were to be written and handed in as an example of what questions would be asked in the interview. The interview was to be taped and then summarized. A tape and detailed summary would be the final project. A researcher's log was to be kept and anonymity of the informant maintained by using a pseudonym.

There were nineteen informants. The interviews revealed surprising results. It was fascinating to see the twists and turns that each informant's life has taken, how agency came into play in some cases, and in others how circumstance intervened to shape the life story. Some, like Jose and Reina (pseudonyms), found that they had to overcome negative stereotypes. Jose was told when he first came that he should shave his moustache in order to be seen as more trustworthy by Americans. Reina, who is from the Dominican Republic, found that even though she learned English and earned a college degree, she was discriminated against because of her accent. She found that men thought her "easy," and employers thought she was not a serious professional. The only job she could get was in the high school she attended where the administrators knew her well. She felt that she never abandoned her Dominican identity.

In the same way, Joseph, an Indian who came from East Africa, felt he still maintained his Indian-African identity. Already a success in the construction business in Kenya, he won a lottery and decided to come to the United States. He regretted that some cultural aspects from his African life were missing. Specifically, he felt his feelings were reduced when he traveled back to Africa to visit: "When I speak, they feel that I am changing, like losing my feelings and emotions." But other aspects of the culture in the United States also bothered Joseph. He found a lack of respect here as opposed to Kenya. He didn't like to hear children speak to their teachers using their first name: "In Kenya you would be sent home for good to learn respect because of that. You can be punished for a long time if you do not know how to address the elderly."

Bharti, an Indian from India, found life much harder than she had expected when she emigrated, hoping for a better career path and opportunity for her son. Money was not being earned to sustain the family, and she went back to India where her husband died. While in India, she improved her English, adjusted her attitude, and became an extrovert, taking the slightest opportunity to make friendships with different segments of the community.

Like Bharti, Francisco was disappointed when he immigrated to the United States. He found the living conditions crowded and depressing. While in the Dominican Republic, he lived in a large house with lots of rooms. He felt that success was difficult to attain and you have to work very hard to achieve it. He said that he had tried to achieve success for ten years but had not reached it yet. His identity was Dominican, and when he married, he promised to raise his children in that culture. However he felt it was important to adapt to this culture here to take advantage of opportunity.

Another immigrant, Esther, came from Cuba at the age of eighteen. Her family was seeking political asylum in Florida. She described a kind of "culture shock" in which even ice cream seemed strange. She found American culture lacking in family values; or at least, not enough emphasis was put on family. Television watching took up people's time instead of conversing with family. Though she was successful in learning English and finished college, she had a good job in Spanish television. She felt that she is Cuban and will always have this basic identity even though she is bilingual and speaks English fluently.

Another interviewee, Danny, came to America from San Salvador. Like Esther, he was a political refugee. His brother was killed during the civil war in his country. Fearing for his life too, he escaped and applied for political asylum. He had been living here for 22 years at the time of the interview.

Determined to learn English, he formed a method of writing everything that he didn't understand in a note pad and looking it up later. As the interviewer quoted Danny:

Deep inside, there is still a Salvadorian pumping, trying to get out. Sometimes, I daydream of those days in my hometown and how it use to be. I remember the hot summer days I spent along my older brother and my three sisters. I remember my father lying in multi-color hammock. My father was playing the guitar and playfully singing for his kids. This moment still lives vividly in my mind. Since I left my native country, I never saw my parents again. I hold on to these memories because it is all I have left from what use to be a close and loving family.

When his parents died, he wasn't able to go to Salvador for the funeral. The loss still lives in his mind.

It is comfortable to judge others when we have it so easy. In America, all individuals have the opportunity to acquire an education. It is up to the individual to take advantage of it. . . . America is the only place where there are people from all over the world looking for a better life. It is a learning experience. Essentially, it is interesting to find out that we are essentially the same.

Danny is a success, having become fully bilingual. He now owns his own business, is married and has two daughters.

Many immigrants had to endure hardships until they could find their work identity here. A Peruvian woman, Rita, had to endure years of working in a Goya food factory, where she said she had to pack beans in plastics bags up to 65 per minute, and clean the place—a tedious and boring job. It was there that she met her husband and a very good friend, Carmen. She worked there for ten years, while attending Jersey City State University. After she got her degree in bilingual education, she took the National Teachers Examination, which she failed many times due to her lack of English before finally passing and getting the job she really wanted. In her interview, Rita thanked her family and friends and said she owed her success to the support she received from them.

Many immigrants find that instead of gaining the sense of agency, they become more dependent. Kiko, who was a teacher in Korea, found herself more dependent when the family immigrated here. Fearful from watching television westerns, she was afraid to go to America, afraid that if she made a mistake in English something bad would happen. She became a housewife dependent on her husband for spending money, something that would never happen in Korea, where the wife controls the purse strings. Kiko also was disappointed in the confusion and identity issues that her children faced when they went to school, returning home to ask "Why am I not American?" Kiko herself began to have doubts about Korean customs she had taken for granted. In many ways her own identity as a Korean woman was shaken by her perception that American women are more attractive than Korean women, and that American people are friendlier. When she returned to Korea, she was appalled by the realization that drinking is a national problem for Korean men, who frequently drink after work. Also, when she returned home, she felt that safety is not enough of an issue because people don't use helmets and car safety belts.

Another Asian, Grace, from Vietnam, felt that her identity changed when she moved. In her native country, conversation with the family was considered very important. In the United States, no one talks much because they work longer hours and everyone is too tired. She switched her work identity from business in which she had a master's degree in her country to computer science because that was the field in which her relatives had found jobs. She was hoping that their support would help her find a job herself.

Maya from Israel felt that her identity became incomplete when she moved here. She felt she lacked roots and was not from either country. She noticed that America's world was safer; she preferred the calmer political life. Israelis are more opinionated and less patient and give their children more independence at an earlier age due to the fact that most mothers are working. They give even small children house keys. She takes a very realistic view of acculturation: "You will always be a stranger to those who were born here. Find at least one good person from your own country whom you can call and talk with."

An artist who put her work on hold due to the fact that she has young children, Maya realized that had she stayed in Israel, she would be more recognized as an artist today.

Many immigrants are embarrassed by how they look or speak. Jose was embarrassed by how he spoke. He believes that "if you are an immigrant you must leave embarrassment in your native country and wear a shield of armor so that you can integrate without much damage to your inner self."

Yet all are grateful for the economic bounty of living in the United States. One interviewee was a poor immigrant, Nick from Italy, who was able to get an operation for a cleft palate, something that would never happen in the poor area where he lived. There, he had no indoor plumbing, and meat was scarce. The harsh conditions influenced the family, and Nick's father would beat him for small infractions like being a few minutes late for dinner. Here in the United States, he felt supported and cared for, and was able to advance to a position of foreman in his job in a municipal agency. He became a U.S. citizen and felt that until you feel you are invested in America and committed, you are not truly an American. He is glad he is an American citizen, but he feels sad when he returns to Italy because he feels he is no longer from there. At the same time, he still feels different from most Americans here.

Beatriz, called "self-motivated and self-aware" by those who know her, is a young woman who feels that when she is with people from her country, Columbia, she is more relaxed and informal. Even though she felt safer here in the United States, she still is not used to the fast lifestyle. She learned enough English to feel that "a new lifestyle is available to her, one in which she would never treat people who do not speak her language the way she was treated." She said that people who speak English were not patient with her when she was learning English and trying to be understood.

Rhaana, a Muslim immigrant, feels safer here than in her native country, Pakistan. However, after September 11, 2001, she has felt pressure to show her religion to be a religion of peace, and the terrorists who attacked New York as "monsters and criminals." Rhaana keeps her cultural habits of dress and family life while trying to coexist peacefully with the new culture. She feels, for example, that marriage is a family matter, as is divorce, and women should keep a demure appearance. She is happy to pursue her goal as teacher, an opportunity she would not have had in her native country.

Here is the summary of an ethnographic interview of Natasha, completed by student Maria Shirta August 7, 2003.

> Natasha Popescu came to this country five years ago when she was in her forties. She came with her husband, Mikhail, and her daughter, Katerina. They came because they won the American lottery. It changed their lives profoundly.
>
> Seven years ago, Natasha read in a Romanian newspaper about the American Lottery and how to take a chance on it. She showed her husband the article, and he just laughed at her. He said, "Do you really think you will win the lottery? In your dreams, my dear!" Nevertheless, she didn't listen and took a chance to win for herself and her family. When they learned they won, that they were selected, it was a terrible shock for the family. They didn't know whether they should be happy or not. It was indeed a chance, a one-in-a-million chance, but they would have to give up everything that made up their lives, including their friends and family. They would go into the unknown, an unfamiliar country whose language they did not speak.
>
> The decision was a tough one. They had a good life in their town in Romania; they had an apartment in town, and two houses their parents owned in a village. They owned a car. But, they thought of their daughter's future, and decided that Katerina would have better opportunities in the United States. So the decision was made to emigrate.
>
> They arrived in New York City in the summer, and what a shock it was for them! Natasha confesses that she really expected the United States to be at least as civilized as Germany which they had visited. They were horrified at how dirty New York City was. They had expected it to be at least as clean as their hometown.
>
> The culture shock took the form of anxiety. They were worried about making a living in New York City, and what the future held in store for them. Would they be sorry they came?

For the first two months, they lived with some friends who had an extra bedroom. Natasha and Mikhail slept in one twin bed and Katerina in another. They tried desperately to find work since their resources they brought from Romania were rapidly being spent. Not speaking English was an impediment in finding a good job. At the beginning, Mikhail accepted a job in a factory at minimum wage ($5.15 an hour), and Natasha took a position as a babysitter for $800 a month. Those were really hard times.

They wished they had never come, but they knew they would not be happy back in Romania either. People would laugh at them or see them as failures. Most of all, no one would believe stories about their hardship.

Gradually, with help from friends and a lot of hard work, they were able to rent an apartment in Queens and furnish it. They bought a PC for Katerina who started school in September. Katerina suffered a lot; she felt she had no friends, and was cut off from friends at home in Romania. When she wrote to them, she didn't want to complain about her difficulties with them.

Luckily, her experience in school saved her from depression. She found she remembered some English from classes for three years in Romanian schools. She didn't like school there, but here in New York City, she found she enjoyed going to school. The curriculum was easier for her here than in Romania. She found she could be a successful student here. Her teachers were very helpful to her in passing standardized tests. She even won in a state contest of web designs because she excelled in computer classes; due to her efforts, her school was judged number one. Her parents were influenced by her success and became more optimistic.

Meanwhile, Natasha who was bilingual, speaking German and Romanian, found learning English to be easy. She was sorry to see her husband, who spoke only Romanian, having difficulties. He was resigned to his factory job, however. She said she felt like a sponge (she actually used that metaphor), picking up words every day. As soon as she would learn them, she would write them down and look them up later in the dictionary. As soon as she learned some English, she went to a business school and got a degree in medical billing.

This was a big step for Natasha. She felt she was getting control of her life. In Romania, she would never have had the opportunity. There she would have been considered too old. There is an age limit for entering college and getting degrees.

Unfortunately, though, she found the amount of money she made was less than she had made as a baby-sitter. She decided that this was because she had little experience and soon she would gain experience and get a better job in the field of medical accounts.

With her success at finding a job in a field she liked, and her daughter's success as a student, Natasha felt optimistic about the future. However, she did not like being so busy: the two jobs left her little time to be with her family. She said that her personality has changed. She is more serious, does not laugh like she used to. She didn't know if she wants to become an American citizen. But when someone told her that she could get financial aid for Natasha to go to college, she decided to plan to apply for citizenship.

Though she has many friends who are Romanian, she does not feel that she is just Romanian. She feels that she is between two cultures, belonging to neither. She visited her native country three years ago. She felt that there was a clash of beliefs as to what it means to live in America. Romanians believe that everyone can get rich quickly in America, forgetting that one has to afford to live in the United States where everything costs a lot, especially rent, taxes, transportation, food, and clothes.

She was unable to convince anyone how hard her life was since she could afford to go anywhere and do anything in Romania with the money she had brought from the United States. However, her family and friends were all thirsty for information about her new life in New York City.

In conclusion, this researcher can say that Natasha has changed a lot. If she compares her life with what it might have been if she had remained in Romania, her life has changed for the better. Now they can even afford to spend one or two family vacations abroad a year. They are doing well economically now. They can even afford to help other Romanian immigrants adjust; they are generous to newcomers.

However, success has come with a price. Natasha no longer has time to cook family meals; they are all gaining weight eating fast and frozen foods. She is dressing like American women and wears pants, which she has mixed feelings about. They celebrate the American holidays and have decided to adopt the optimistic and practical American attitude. They know they will have a bright, happy future here.

They try not to think about the part of themselves they left behind and the price they paid, but rather continue to build on their good fortune in a "land of opportunity." When they look at their daughter, who is now in graduate school, they are sure they made the right decision to come to the United States.

In summary, the informants whose interviews have been summarized or presented as examples here have presented several themes or underlying ideas. Obviously these themes are merely topics that need more interviews, and more naturalistic research, for further exploration.

1. There are opportunities professionally and economically available here for immigrants. They are particularly happy that their children have educational and economic opportunities here.
2. Working longer and harder than before, they have less time than before to spend with family.
3. Immigrants, like Americans, have become consumers and eat more fast food. Sometimes this impacts their health, and they gain weight.
4. They feel safer here than in their native country.
5. Immigrants feel prejudice because of their language and their appearance.
6. When they go home, they feel a sense of *anomie.* They no longer fit in their native country, yet in the United States they are made to feel different so that they don't fit in here either.
7. Even though most immigrants are glad to learn English for practical and personal reasons, they feel that they will also maintain a membership in the native culture through language.
8. Although some feel that Americans are friendly people, some immigrants feel that they were not patient toward them as they attempted to communicate in English as a second language.
9. The immigrants who make it are those who have support from family. Those who don't have support from family must find a social network to help them adjust.

The Valdéz Family

I met a Mexican family, the Valdéz family, when I offered my services as translator to The Interreligious Fellowship for the Homeless at the family shelter in Englewood, New Jersey. I first met the mother, Maria (not her real name), who came here to avoid abuse from her spouse, an alcoholic. Not having time to wait for a visa and fearing for her life and the well-being of her daughters, she came across the border illegally with her three daughters, the youngest of whom was five years old, and went through hardships in the crossing. She was even arrested at one point and sent to jail; she was released after an overnight there due to the illness of one of her daughters, an experience she remembers with tears in her eyes.

Not knowing much English, Maria found it difficult to find work. Since Maria was attractive and personable, she soon found opportunities. After working as a maid, a job that gave her time to learn enough English to get by, she sold shoes at Sears using a false identification card. She lived in a homeless shelter while her daughters went to a local school where they learned English rapidly and did well. At the shelter, she was able to save her money, and after a few months, she went into transitional housing supported by a county agency. At this time she met a Mexican man, Mario, who had a steady job as a chef in an Italian restaurant in Plainfield. For a time with both of them working, they were able to pay the bills and the family stabilized.

Then, marital discord created a downward slide that undermined Maria's health and spirit. Mario, who had been very generous with both his money and his time and seemed genuinely fond of Maria's daughters, became domineering and demonstrated the male-dominant attitude of "machismo" as soon as they were married. He would not let Maria or her daughters go anywhere, keeping them at home like prisoners. They had become accustomed to the freedom American women enjoy. The daughters, intelligent and attractive, became sullen and withdrawn as they watched their American counterparts go to parks and school functions. Maria had to leave her job in shoes due to a degenerative condition in her spine. She was planning to undergo back surgery and then separate from Mario when the INS came into their apartment and imprisoned Mario, giving Maria 30 days to go back to Mexico.

In this interview, I asked Maria how this made her feel. I used techniques from ethnographic interviews (see Chapter 6).

Interviewer: How did this make you feel after all of this to realize the one thing that you had feared, the Immigration Service finding you and your family, had finally happened?

Maria: I was sad. More than anything, I felt bad because of the way they treated us, like criminals.

I: I agree. You are good people, the kind that this country should have. I am sorry you were made to feel this way. What will happen to your youngest daughter Lucy?

M: She will decide whether to finish high school here or in South Carolina with her sister.

The two older daughters, having graduated high school, have both married American citizens and are applying for residency. However, because of recent shifts in the immigration laws, even if an illegal immigrant marries a citizen, it is a long process and the couple could even be separated and the daughter sent back to Mexico for a period of time. They felt as if they were being punished for a crime they didn't commit because they came here as children and were not in charge of their identities and their lives.

The fact is, the future looks bleak for Maria. In Mexico, she will not be able to afford the surgery she needs that will allow her to work. And, if her youngest daughter remains here in the United States, Maria will be alone.

Maria is estranged from her family in Mexico and has few close friends there. A friend she met in New Jersey is trying to arrange for work for her in the Cancun area in a hotel. A transcript of an ethnographic interview follows that I conducted with Maria's oldest daughter, Nadia, who is twenty-two and living in Virginia with her husband who is in the Marines. Her sister Nuris lives with them, and Lucy is with an aunt in Teaneck where she attends high school. As you read the interview, please notice how questions are designed to elicit information about Nadia; they are open-ended to encourage as much verbalization as possible from the informant. As always, the name of the informant has been changed to protect privacy.

Interviewer: Why did you come from Mexico? From which city?

Nadia: We came in 1993 from Mexico City. My father was a cop in Mexico and abusing my mother; he even incarcerated her, trying to get permanent custody of us. We could not go to the police and get protection, so my mother decided to leave the country.

I: How did you immigrate? What point did you go into this country?

N: Tijuana. We tried to cross, but the police got us and were going to put us in jail for 24 hours, but Lucy got sick and they had to let us go after a few hours.

I: Where did you go after that? Tell me about it.

N: Secaucus, New Jersey, where mom thought a job was waiting that a boyfriend who lived there had gotten for her. This turned out to be only for a few months because the plan didn't work out.

I: How did you like school there? How did you find learning English?

N: It was very difficult. We didn't know much at all; we were very quiet girls and people made fun of us. There weren't a lot of Spanish-speaking students in the class. I remember the teacher thought I was incapable of passing so she told me to copy the student in front of me. Once we had a test, and she told me to copy. The student performed poorly, and I didn't like my grade. So I asked if I could take the test for real, not copying. I made a good grade, but the teacher didn't believe it was deserved, and made me take it again. I made a good grade again and finally she believed it, but I still felt I didn't get what I deserved.

I: Could you have gone to the ESL teacher and complained? Was she a good teacher?

N: Yes, but we were good girls and we were taught to be quiet and behave.

I: How did you learn this?

N: Our mother was very strict and in Mexico, so was our grandmother.

I: Then what happened?

N: We went to Texas and lived with relatives. I liked the school there. We learned a lot of English that year.

I: They probably had a lot of English language learners there.

N: Yes, but then we went back to New Jersey and to the shelter in Englewood where we went to school in Hackensack when we were in transitional housing, we went to Teaneck. We liked the schools there and the community. We would have been different people if we had stayed there.

I: Because of the teacher, or because it was middle-class?

N: Both. It was very nice.

I: How do you feel about your mother being sent back to Mexico?

N: Terrible, but if she is happy finally, it will be okay.

I: She and Mario will stay separated?

N: Yes.

I: Has all this moving around affected you and your sisters?

N: Well, it has affected my sister Nuris in that she can't express her emotion; she keeps it all bottled up inside. And Lucy is a very sad person. She longs to go back to Teaneck, which makes her think of happier days.

I: Will you become an American citizen?

N: Definitely. But I have to wait until the lawyer tells me. I will have to send them information about coming here illegally as children, and we have to wait to get a residency.

I: Can they deny you because you came illegally, even though you were children and not in control of your lives?

N: Yes, but I am hoping they will allow me to stay. I will be willing to go back to Mexico for a short time if that will help me become legal.

I: What are your plans for the future?

N: I will go to college and get a degree in Business.

I: What do you want for your children?

N: I want a happy home, free from fear and violence.

I: What have you learned from your experience?

N: That Americans do not know how lucky they are, and they take their freedom and opportunity for granted. We have seen American schoolmates taking drugs and dropping out of school. It makes us sad when we would love to have the opportunities that they obviously take for granted.

I: I hope you will realize all your dreams, Nadia. Thank you for this interview.

Source: Field Notes Interview Journal, January 12, 2005.

In the experience of interviewing the Valdéz family, the issue of the "hyphenated" Americans and their identity is central to the story. The Valdéz family, Maria and her daughters, were seeking asylum and truly were in exile. They needed sanctuary from abuse, as do many immigrants who come here illegally. I have found that my students find it very unfair that this family should be punished for being hard-working, moral people, when there are hardened criminals who commit crimes that warrant punishment. For example, we have given asylum to women from Africa who were threatened with genital mutilation, so why can't we find a way to help people like Maria and her daughters? These are subjective issues, of course, but you can see how the ethnographic interviews awaken new perspectives for students—they hear real-life stories about people, stories they never imagined were true.

Questions for Discussion and Writing
1. What is particularly striking about the interviews of the Valdéz family?
2. What do you think are implications for our immigration policy? What should our government policy be for individuals exiled from their country because of dangerous situations, either from politics or family?
3. If you could speak to the immigrants in this chapter, what would you say?
4. What insight did you gain about teaching English from Nadia's interview?
5. Summarize what you have learned about the ethnographic interview. Use the interviews in this chapter as examples.

LITERARY INTERVIEWS

In addition to ethnographic interviews, literary interviews have been conducted that reveal the identity and culture of bilingual writers. In *Puerto Rican Voices in English: Interviews with Writers* by Carmen Dolores Hernandez, she uncovers feelings by bilingual Puerto Rican writers who write about their identity as people and as writers. One writer, Esmeralda Santiago, says:

> *Everyone is trying to hold on to the culture they had. Your culture is your identity. . . . I don't think there is an American sense of identity, not in the urban areas. I think this kind of thing is conscious choice. There is that attitude that you are going to hold on to what makes you different, what separates you rather than to what brings you together. (Hernandez, 1997, p. 157)*

The Puerto Rican identity is an example of how complicated identity can get. Rather than one identity, there is a constellation of identities, like the poet Louis Reyes Rivera, who articulates the differences between Puerto Ricans from the island and those from the mainland, maintains. He says that islanders treat those who return from, say, New York as not authentic Puerto Ricans, and New York Puerto Ricans have to deal with another prejudice—that of racism. According to Rivera, although Puerto Ricans are technically part of the United States, they are not treated that way there. He says much of the Nuyorican poetry is rooted in African identity, and the young Lords fashioned themselves after the black panthers (Hernandez, 1997, p. 119).

Another writer, Abraham Rodriguez, calls himself both an American and a Puerto Rican. He typifies the shift between the younger and older generation of writers. He feel the term "Hispanos" is misleading and refers to Spain, which many Puerto Ricans feel is a place unrelated to their reality. Rodriguez, whose book sold 18,000 copies and was optioned for a movie, feels that writing provided a way to define his identity and find success both financially and personally. When he speaks at high schools, he encourages young people to express themselves, and he uses his life as an example (Hernandez, 1997, p. 137).

Miguel Algarín, founder of the famous Nuyorican Café in Manhattan, feels that one should not have a conflict between a love of English literature and the culture of Puerto Rico. He felt that the two interests have enriched his life and calls himself a Shakepearean scholar. Algarin founded the Nuyorican Café so that Puerto Ricans could have an audience for their self-expression. Algarin has published two anthologies with Miguel Pinero and his legacy, the Nuyorican Café, continues to be a unique cultural landmark in New York City (Hernandez, 1997, p. 33).

> ### Question for Discussion and Writing
>
> Invite a bilingual writer to your class, then interview him or her as to what feelings of identity surface in the writing.

Epilogue: Identity and Home

Exile is a universal experience and one that is more and more common as the globalization of the world economy intensifies. Border crossing has become more and more idealized in the media in films and literature. As entertainment this can be exciting, but the fantasy of the exiled hero or heroine with the accompanying angst and anomie can be far from the truth of the individual struggle to find agency and authenticity in a new context, a new life.

I have discussed the cost to the individual in the struggle to acculturate in *Lives in Two Languages* (University of Michigan Press, 2001). I am impressed by the flexibility that a person can have in fashioning a new identity and making the best out of circumstances that are not within the individual's control.

It is true that the objectivity of perspective gained by exile can be a resource, especially for writers, beginning with Conrad and Nabokov and continuing with modern writers, like Kyoko Mori, Isabel Allende, V.S. Naipaul, and many more than we have been able to include in this book. This resource can be seen as the positive end of a spectrum that includes frustration and loss. The yearning for home and security exists alongside the lure of the exotic and the unknown. We are never completely home in terms of being completely safe. Uncertainty and danger will always exist, especially in this day and age. Home can become idealized or demonized, and thus lead to extremes in attitude and thinking. Reason must intervene; when we learn something new, we are visiting a new place, even if it is in our minds. Landmarks cannot be fixed symbols in our thinking but points of reference in a world community. We can integrate the new into the old and make transitions more gradual as we move into new territory.

It has been said that writers carry their home, even their identities, on their backs, that their writing creates a true home for them. As someone who writes, I can attest to that fact. And when I go back to my oldest home, I do not find that I can write because the perspective and objectivity of it have gone. I am too busy living that life, like a pair of slippers that feel very comfortable.

Mary Catherine Bateson says that we are all immigrants today because we are learning to live in a world we are not familiar with and we must "live lightly on the earth and to hold our convictions lightly too; to go against the ancient impulse to maximize our offspring and our accumulation and our years of life. To take care of one another in spite of profound differences" (Bateson, 134–135). I believe we must learn from our stories and take responsibility when we can to shape them in positive, life-affirming ways. In this direction lies our true home.

Appendix A

Films that would be appropriate for study regarding identity and acculturation are:

1. *El Norte* (1983)
2. *Green Card* (1990)
3. *The House of Sand and Fog* (2003)
4. *In America* (2002)
5. *In the Time of the Butterflies* (2001)
6. *The Joy Luck Club* (1993)
7. *Lone Star* (1996)
8. *Maria Full of Grace* (2004)
9. *Mi Familia (My Family)* (1995)
10. *Moscow on the Hudson* (1984)
11. *Osama* (2003)
12. *Spanglish* (2004)
13. *The Terminal* (2004)

Appendix B

To Whom It May Concern:

I hereby give permission to use this interview for research purposes.
I understand that my name will be changed to protect my privacy.

Signed: _____

Bibliography

Aciman, A. (Ed.) (1999). *Letters of transit: Reflection on exile, identity, language and loss.* New York: The New York Public Library.

Agar, M. (1980). *The professional stranger: An informal introduction to ethnography.* New York: Academic Press.

Akhtar, S. (1995). A third individuation: Immigration, identity, and the psychoanalytic process. *Journal of the American Psychoanalytic Association, 43*(4), 1051–1009.

Allende, I. (2003). *My invented country: A nostalgic journey through Chile* (M. S. Peden, Trans.). New York: HarperCollins.

Alvarez, J. (1998). *Something to declare.* New York: Algonquin Books of Chapel Hill.

Anzaldúa, G. (1987). To live in the borderlands means you. In *Borderlands/La frontera: The new mestizo.* San Francisco: Aunt Lute Books.

Arana, M. (2001). *American chica: Two worlds, one childhood.* New York: Dial Press.

Bakhtin, M. (1981). *The dialogic imagination: Four essays by M.M. Bakhtin* (M. Holquist, Ed., & C. Emerson, Trans.). Austin, TX: University of Texas Press.

Bateson, M.C. (2000). *Full circle, overlapping lives: Culture and generation in transition.* New York: Random House.

Bruchas, J. (1979). Ellis Island. In G. Hobson (Ed.), *The remembered earth.* Albuquerque, NM: Red Earth Press.

Bruner, J. (1991). The narrative construction of reality. *Critical Inquiry, 18,* 1–21.

Chomsky, N. (1972). *Language and mind.* New York: Harcourt.

Codrescu, A. (1998). *Hail Babylon: In search of the American city at the end of the millennium.* New York: Saint Martin's Press.

———. (2003). How I got to America. In *It was today.* Minneapolis, MN: Coffee House Press.

Conway, J.K. (1969). *The road from Coorain.* New York: Alfred Knopf.

———. (1970). *True north.* New York: Alfred Knopf.

———. (1999). *When memory speaks: Exploring the art of autobiography.* New York: Vintage Books.

Cottingham, J. (Ed.) (1992). *The Cambridge companion to Descartes.* Cambridge: Cambridge University Press.

Donaldson, M. (1978). *Children's minds.* New York: W.W. Norton.

Flores-Gonzalez, N. (2002). *School kids/street kids.* New York: Columbia University Press.

Florio-Ruane, S. (2001). *Teacher education and the cultural imagination: Autobiography, conversation, and narrative.* Mahwah, NJ: Lawrence Erlbaum.

Frost, R. (1969). The road not taken. In *The poetry of Robert Frost.* New York: Henry Holt.

Geertz, C. (1973). *The interpretation of cultures.* New York: Basic Books.

———. (2000). *Available light: Anthropological reflections on philosophical topics.* Princeton, NJ: Princeton University Press.

Gilligan, C. (1977). In a different voice: Women's conception of self and of morality. *Harvard Educational Review, 47,* 481–517.

———. (1993). *In a different voice.* Cambridge, MA: Harvard University Press.

Gilligan, C., & Brown, L.M. (1992). *Meeting at the crossroads.* Cambridge, MA: Harvard University Press.

Goffman, E. (1959). *The presentation of the self in everyday life.* New York: Doubleday.

Goleman, D. (1985). *Vital lies, simple truths: The psychology of self-deception.* New York: Simon and Shuster.

Hakuta, K. (1986). *Mirror of language: The debate on bilingualism.* New York: Basic Books.

Hernandez, C. (1997). *Puerto Rican voices in English: Interviews with writers.* Westport, CT: Praeger.

Hoffman, E. (1989). *Lost in translation: A life in a new language.* New York: Penguin Books.

———. (2001). *The secret.* New York: Ballantine Books.

Howe, I. (1976). *World of our fathers: The Journey of the East European Jews to America and the life they made and found.* New York: Harcourt.

Ivanic, R., & Camps, D. (2001). I am how I sound: Voice as self-representation in L2 writing. *Journal of Second Language Writing, 10,* 3–33.

Kemper, S. (1984). The development of narrative skills: Explanations and entertainments. In S. Kuczaj (Ed.), *Discourse development: Progress in cognitive development research, Vol. 2.* (pp. 99–124). New York: Springer.

Lahiri, J. (2004). *The namesake.* New York: Houghton Mifflin, Inc.

Levi-Strauss, C. (1958). *Structural anthropology* (C. Jacobson & B. Schoept, Trans.). New York: Basic Books.

Lofland, J., & Lofland, L. (1984). *Analyzing social settings: A guide to qualitative observation and analysis.* Belmont, CA: Wadsworth.

Lopate, P. (1987). *The rug merchant.* New York: Viking Penguin.

McBride, J. (1996). *The color of water.* New York: Riverhead Books.

Mead, G.H. (1977). *George Herbert Mead on social psychology. Selected papers* (A. Strauss, Ed.). Chicago: University of Chicago Press.

Mernissi, F. (1994). *Dreams of trespass: Tales of a harem girlhood.* New York: Washington Square Press.

———. (2001). *Scheherazade goes west: Different cultures, different harems.* New York: Washington Square Press.

Mora, P. (1984). Elena. In *Chants.* Houston: Arte-Publico Press, University of Houston.

Morales, A.L. (1986). Child of the Americas. In *Getting home alive.* Ithaca, NY: Firebrand Books.

Mori, K. (1997). *Polite lies: On being a woman caught between cultures.* New York: Fawcett Books.

Nafisi, A. (2004). *Reading Lolita in Tehran: A memoir in books.* New York: Random House.

Naipaul, V.S. (2001). *Half a life.* New York: Vintage Books.

Neisser, U. (1976). *Cognition and reality.* San Francisco: Freeman.

Neruda, P. (2003). I will come back/Yo volvere. In I. Stavans (Ed.), *The poetry of Pablo Neruda.* New York: Farrar, Strauss & Giroux.

Obama, B. (1995). *Dreams from my father: A story of race and inheritance.* New York: Three Rivers Press.

Ogulnick, K. (2000). *Language crossings: Negotiating the self in a multicultural world.* New York: Teacher College Press.

Pavlenko, A., & Lantolf, J. (2000). Second language learning as participation and reconstruction of selves. In *Sociocultural theory and second language learning* (pp. 155–178). Oxford: Oxford University Press.

Piaget, J. (1952). *The origins of intelligence in children.* New York: International Universities Press, Inc.

Polkinghorne, D.E. (1988). *Narrative knowing and the human sciences.* Albany, NY: State University of New York Press.

Quiñones, E. (2000). *Bodega dreams.* New York: Vintage Press.

Schumann, F., & Schumann, J. (1977). Diary of a language learner: An introspective study of second language learning. In H.D. Brown, R. Crymes, & C. Yorio (Eds.), *Teaching and learning: Trends in research and practice.* Washington, DC: TESOL.

Sfard, A. (1998). On two metaphors for learning and the dangers of choosing just one. *Educational Researcher, 27,* 4–13.

Shiebe, K. (1986). Self-narratives and adventure. In T.R. Sarbin (Ed.), *Narrative psychology: The storied nature of human conduct* (pp. 129–151). New York: Praeger.

Silko, L.M. (1981). Where the mountain lion lay down with the deer. In *Storyteller*. New York: Seaver Books.

Smith, Z. (2000). *White teeth*. New York: Vintage International.

Song, C. (1983). Lost sister. In *Picture bride*. New Haven, CT: Yale University Press.

Spradley, J. (1979). *The ethnographic interview*. New York: Holt, Rinehart and Winston.

Tan, A. (1989). *The joy luck club*. New York: Penguin Books.

———. (2003). *The opposite of fate: Memories of a writing life*. New York: Penguin Books.

Tran, B. (2002). Love and rice. In *In the mynah bird's own words* (p. 3). Dorset, VT: Tupelo Press.

Trounstine, J. (2004). *Shakespeare behind bars: One teacher's story of the power of drama in a women's prison*. Ann Arbor: University of Michigan Press.

Vygotsky, L.S. (1978). *Mind in society*. Cambridge, MA: Harvard University Press.

Walcott, D. (1987). A far cry from Africa. In *Collected poems, 1948–1984*. New York: Farrar, Straus & Giroux.

Watkins-Goffman, L. (2001). *Lives in two languages: An exploration of identity and culture*. Ann Arbor: University of Michigan Press.

Wertsch, J.V. (1991). *Voices of the mind: A sociocultural approach to mediated action*. Cambridge, MA: Harvard University Press.

Yun, M. (2004). *Translations of beauty*. New York: Atria Books.

Acknowledgments

Grateful acknowledgment is given to the following graduate students in my class of Applied Linguistics at Jersey City State University whose projects were mentioned in this book: Denise Adams, Yoleisy Alvarez, Colleen Amador, Nelly Berrios-Urena, Lucille Camp, Enid Collazo, Claudia Echavarria-McCurdy, Everlydis Falcon-Duran, Sharon Kramer, Frank Manzo, Ketsia Mesidor, Liliana Ortiz, Jaya Poojary, Wilkin Pujols, Jacqueline Richard, Tracey Dunn Roodenburg, Betsy Rosario, Yanira Segovia, Maria Shirta, and Patricia Ward.

I would also like to gratefully acknowledge the support that Kelly Sippell and the staff at the University of Michigan Press have given me during the writing of this text.

Grateful acknowledgment is given to the following authors, publishers, and individuals for permission to reprint their materials or previously published materials.

Arte Publico Press for "Elena" from *Chants* by Pat Mora. Copyright © 1985 Arte Publico Press–University of Houston. Reprinted with permission.

The Perseus Book Group for material from *Dreams of Trespass: Tales of a Harem Girlhood* by Fatima Mernissi. Copyright © 1994 by Fatima Mernissi. Reprinted by permission of Perseus Books PLC, a member of Perseus Books, L.L.C.

Random House, Inc. for material from *White Teeth* by Zadie Smith. Copyright © 2000 by Zadie Smith. Used by permission of Random House, Inc.

Random House, Inc., for material from *Half a Life* by V. S. Naipul. Copyright © 2001 by V. S. Naipul. Used by permission of Alfred A. Knopf, a division of Random House, Inc.

Seaver Books for "Where Mountain Lion Lay Down with Deer" from *Storyteller* by Leslie Marmon Silko. Copyright © 1981 by Leslie Marmon Silko, published by Seaver Books, New York, New York.

Tupelo Press for "Love and Rice" from *In the Mynah Bird's Own Words* by Barbara Tran. Copyright © 2002.

White Pine Press for "I Will Come Back/Yo Volvere" by Pablo Neruda.

Yale University Press for "Lost Sister" from *Picture Bride* by Cathy Song. Copyright © 1983 Yale University Press. Reprinted with permission.

Every effort has been made to contact the copyright holders for permission to reprint borrowed material. We regret any oversights that may have occurred and will rectify them in future printings of this book.

Index